# Pioneering the Helicopter

A GLIMPSE INTO THE FUTURE?

The author's children pose in the VS-300 after the first actual back-yard landing (see page 139).

# Pioneering the Helicopter

## CHARLES LESTER MORRIS

Consultant to Sikorsky Aircraft
Division of United Technologies Corporation
Formerly:    Chief Test Pilot, Field Service Manager,
Sikorsky Aircraft;
Director of Field Operations,
Bendix Helicopter Inc.;
Demonstration and Training Pilot,
Eastern Distributor of Hiller Helicopters;
Field Service Manager & Asst. Vice President
Kaman Aircraft Corp.

HELICOPTER ASSOCIATION INTERNATIONAL
Alexandria -------------------------------------------Virginia

*This book is produced in full compliance
with the government's regulations for con-
serving paper and other essential materials*

# *PREFACE*
### *to the*
### *40 Anniversary Edition*

When this book was first published in 1945, it recorded the details of early helicopter developments with particular emphasis on the first Sikorsky models—the now-famous VS-300 and the XR-4, as well as the XR-5 and XR-6. It came fresh from the mind of the author who was in the pilot's seat during those exploratory efforts. It chronicled the "little failures and little successes . . . gropings in the dark followed by sure-footed progress when a momentary gleam of light appeared".

In 1945, few people knew what a helicopter was or what it might be capable of doing. Even less were directly involved with helicopters. As a result, fewer than 3000 copies were sold, and even fewer exist today. Thus, many people who may now be interested in knowing more about the birth and the fascinating early development of the helicopter may be deprived of this opportunity.

Today, hundreds of thousands of people are directly or indirectly involved in the manufacture or operation of helicopters throughout the world. This 40th anniversary edition is dedicated to them, with the greatest admiration and respect for what they, and their predecessors during the last 40 years, have been able to build on the fragile beginnings recorded here.

Dreams are what the world is built on. Two dreams are reflected in this book.

One dream (mine) is depicted in the fronticepiece: the VS-300 helicopter in my own backyard in Stratford, Connecticut; and also in the final chapter, "Prophesy and Warning". My dream for the helicopter was a vehicle for *personal* flight! I came close to realizing that dream when, in 1949 to 1951, as pilot for the eastern distributor of Hiller Helicopters, I flew the Hiller 360 out of White Plains, New York, and operated in and out of backyards, tennis courts, roadside restaurants, motels, gas stations, my family's summer cottage at the beach, and many other such locations. The further exploration of my dream was cut short by the Korean conflict when all helicopter production was conscripted by the military "for the duration".

That same Korean conflict brought Igor Sikorsky's dream to fulfilment. His dream for the helicopter was, among other things, that it could be an important, or perhaps essential, vehicle for saving lives! His dream was far more realistic than mine.

I recall in 1951 when our paths happened to cross, one Sunday afternoon, on Route 25 between Bridgeport and Newtown, Connecticut. Igor Sikorsky happily signalled me to the side of the highway, jumped out of his car and bounced back to mine. His old-world courteous greetings to my wife and children having been properly rendered, he turned to me with the greatest satisfaction and pride and said, ''Les, our dreams are realized. They are calling our helicopters 'angels of mercy' ''!

Helicopters have continued to be angels of mercy during the years thereafter. By latest count, well over 100,000 lives have been saved by the helicopter. Igor Sikorsky's dream came true during his lifetime.

This anniversary edition of the beginnings of the helicopter is made possible through the sponsorship and support of

Helicopter Association International
Alexandria, Virginia

to whom the author extends his deep appreciation. It is assembled and printed exactly as it was in 1945 when wartime restrictions dictated many details such as the width of margins and the arrangement of photographs. The final chapter, ''Prophesy and Warning'', is retained also, even though it may now stir some chuckles! But it is a reflection of asperations, 40 years ago, at the dawn of the helicopter era.

C. L. (Les) Morris
Westbrook, Conn.
December, 1985

# PREFACE

When the Encyclopaedia Britannica is wrong, that's news. In its 1937 edition, we learn that a helicopter is "extravagant of power. In the light of modern knowledge, one horsepower cannot be expected to lift more than about 15 lb. The whole of the power of a modern commercial aeroplane arranged as a helicopter would be needed merely to sustain it, leaving nothing to raise or propel it."

Thus we are led to believe that a helicopter is impractical. Yet this very conclusion is founded on a misunderstanding of one of the helicopter's basic principles: that it requires *less* horsepower to move forward than it does to hover over one spot.

If the Encyclopaedia erred in its concept of the helicopter, it is little wonder that the casual reader and non-technical layman who do not have access to specialized sources of information should be confused in trying to comprehend this new air vehicle which has burst so abruptly upon our national scene. Their confusion is doubly confounded by the claims and counterclaims that well-meaning but usually uninformed persons have poured forth.

The author has been privileged to witness the development of the Sikorsky helicopter from its inception; indeed, as its chief test pilot from 1941 to 1944, he has been intimately concerned with its welfare. It is his considered opinion that, in order to evaluate just what the helicopter is and what it is not, a knowledge of how it came into being is essential.

It is proposed, therefore, in the following pages, to unfold the tale. It is full of little failures and little successes, stories and anecdotes, gropings in the dark followed by sure-footed progress when a momentary gleam of light appeared. But into it all are woven the courage and tenacity of the man whose name will forever be almost synonymous with *helicopter*—Igor I. Sikorsky.

Many other names are included: names of coworkers and associates whose energies and abilities were applied unstintingly to this development. But unfortunately, it has not been possible in all cases to work the individuals into the story. The author tenders his apology to those whose names have been omitted in deference to continuity. Particular reference is made to A. A. Nikolsky (now Associate Professor of Aeronautical Engineering), who was Assistant to the Chief of Design during the early period of the author's association with the project, and whose clear-cut, analytical pessimism was often responsible for reviewing something that might otherwise have remained a source of personal hazard to the test pilot and of general detriment to the project.

Also, the author presents the following students of his who, in company with those mentioned in the text, comprise the group of intrepid pioneers who dared to take instruction from one who scarcely knew what he essayed to teach:

Lt. Comdr. E. A. H. Peat, Royal Navy, and Flight Lt. F. J. Cable, Royal Air Force, who complete the roster of the author's British students after Wing Comdr. R. A. C. Brie, Royal Air Force.

James G. Ray, America's foremost Autogiro test pilot, whom the author was privileged to train on helicopters, and who still holds top honors for requiring the least amount of instruction before soloing.

D. D. "Jimmie" Viner, who joined the piloting staff early in 1943 and in one brief year was able to assume the duties of Chief Test Pilot.

C. A. "Connie" Moeller, who came with the company just after Viner, and whose engineering training coupled with

*Preface*

piloting skill has already contributed greatly to the progress of the helicopter and has earned him the position of Senior Engineering Test Pilot.

Charles A. Lindbergh, who soloed the VS-300 under the author's tutelage, having had no opportunity to become acquainted with helicopter techniques in a dual-controlled craft.

Lt. Comdr. C. T. Booth, U.S.N., who joined Lt. Comdr. F. A. Erickson of the U.S. Coast Guard to become one of the first two helicopter pilots for the Navy.

In addition, the author wishes to acknowledge his indebtedness to the following:

Michael D. Buivid, without whose accurate records the early history would lack authenticity.

W. Laurence LePage and Prof. Alexander Klemin, for the photographs of early helicopters.

Dr. J. A. J. Bennett, eminent rotary-wing expert, Leslie E. Neville, editor of *Aviation*, and Ralph H. McClarren, Associate Director of The Franklin Institute, all three of whom painstakingly reviewed the original manuscript and thus added immeasurably to its value.

United Aircraft Corporation, for the photographs of the Sikorsky helicopters reproduced herein.

C. L. MORRIS.

*Stratford, Conn.*
*December,* 1944.

# INTRODUCTION

Our organization, which produced the first practical trans-oceanic flying clippers and which recently developed the successful helicopter, has been located in Bridgeport, Connecticut, since 1930. My activity as engineering manager brought me in contact with Mr. C. L. Morris, who was Commissioner of Aeronautics for the state of Connecticut during the ten years from 1931 to 1941. Mr. Morris was known as a resourceful, competent, and resolute State Commissioner, trusted and respected by all the men connected with flying in the state of Connecticut, where he contributed greatly to the safety, as well as to the progress, of civil flying.

In 1939, having resumed my work with helicopters, I had a very interesting discussion with Mr. Morris about this new project. At that time the helicopter was practically non-existent in America and there were very little information, little understanding, and almost no anticipation of the potential value of direct-lift aircraft. I was, therefore, very much impressed by the way in which Mr. Morris understood and appreciated this generally unknown problem. He recognized at once both the difficult and novel nature of the helicopter and its nearly boundless future possibilities.

From that time on it was my earnest desire to invite Mr. Morris to join our engineering department in connection with the helicopter development. In March, 1941, this was accomplished and soon afterward he assumed the duties of chief test pilot. It took him a remarkably short time to familiarize himself with the details of this problem, to learn to fly the helicopter, and quickly to surpass my flying skill and that of another engineer. We two had been until then the only pilots flying this novel aircraft.

The next year Mr. Morris conducted all flight tests of the first helicopter produced for the Army and in May, 1942, delivered it by air from Bridgeport to Dayton, Ohio. This was the first cross-country flight ever made by a helicopter in the Western Hemisphere and, so far as I know, it was by far the longest flight ever accomplished by one in the world. It is hardly necessary to stress that the successful accomplishment of these duties necessitated a thorough knowledge of the helicopter.

Mr. Morris has an outstanding record of flight tests on new-model helicopters. At the time of writing this book, he had to his credit more helicopter flying hours than any other man. The "firsts" to his credit are too numerous to list in detail, but they include the first helicopter flight to exceed 100 miles per hour, the first helicopter flight in America to exceed 5,000 feet in altitude, the first helicopter night flights, the first back-yard landings, the first helicopter roof-top landings, and the first actual power-off landings with a helicopter.

To state that Mr. Morris is very familiar with the subject would therefore be correct, but insufficient. It would be more to the point to state that he was one of the few persons whose ability, persistence, and knowledge helped to make the whole subject of this discussion a reality. I feel that there could be no background or experience that would better qualify a man to discuss the helicopter.

Igor I. Sikorsky.

*December,* 1944.

# CONTENTS

# Contents

## Chapter 1

## IN RETROSPECT

IGOR SIKORSKY'S DINNER CONVERSATION HAD SHUTTLED briskly between history and prophecy. We were relaxing at the Dearborn Inn, across the street from the Ford Airport where the VS-300 helicopter was sheltered for the night. Tomorrow, October 7, 1943, would be the last day her wheels would leave the ground.

Only four years earlier, she had taken off for her first so-called *flight*. In that brief space of time, she had emerged from the status of "Igor's nightmare," had slowly converted critics to staunch admirers by her ever-expanding series of incredible flying accomplishments, had set the country and the world aflame in anticipation of a new, revolutionary means of transportation, and had ended her career by being accorded a permanent niche in the Edison Institute Museum. A "museum piece" after only four years of life!

It was natural that we should spend this last evening reviewing the VS-300's career. She had been very close to us—and we to her. Mr. Sikorsky had had two years more of her childhood than I, so I pressed with careful insistence for details of those early days. But generally, his analytical accuracy permitted him to answer only, "I do not remember exactly. I should have to refer to the photographs. There have been such a multitude of changes!"

Such a multitude of changes! They crowd the memory and clamor for recognition before the doors of progress close forever on a famous aircraft and only dimming recollections are left. Mr. Sikorsky has often said that this experimental baby is not at all the same helicopter that he flew for the first time four years ago. Eighteen major revisions and countless hundreds of minor ones have been incorporated in it. It has evolved, somewhat as the human body evolves, by shedding and renewing cells until, after a period of time, none of the original cells remains at all.

The VS-300 can boast, though, that six items have survived —the seat, the two landing wheels, the box for the transmission, the central fuselage framework, and the gas tank! These parts were with Mr. Sikorsky for his first helicopter take-off, four years ago, and are still there at his last landing before the ship goes to rest among the historic aircraft in the museum.

Such a multitude of changes!

"How did you feel," I asked, "the first time the helicopter left the ground? Were you satisfied or disappointed?"

"Both," he replied. "Of course there were some hopes and dreams that she would float into the air under beautiful control; but dreams seldom come true. She was rough on the controls. She vibrated badly. I got shaken up on the ground and in the air. They say I was just one big blur. The ship was under-powered, so that she would hop off and then settle back down after only a second or two.

"But then—she was new and so was I. It was necessary not only to investigate the aircraft, but also to train myself to fly it. Nobody could tell me how. I just had to learn."

"What were the others doing?" I asked. I knew that Bob Labensky was on hand for these first flights. He was one of the five original employees of the Sikorsky Aero Engineering Corporation in this country, dating back to the spring of 1923. The Gluhareff brothers, Serge and Michael, were there too—they had joined Sikorsky in his very early struggles. I could guess that Michael Buivid was with them because he and Labensky were inseparable partners in any new, experi-

MR. SIKORSKY MAKES THE FINAL FLIGHT IN THE VS-300 (DEARBORN, MICHIGAN; OCTOBER 7, 1943).

THE AUTHOR DEMONSTRATES THE VS-300 IN FRONT OF THE EDISON
INSTITUTE MUSEUM.

THE LAST FLIGHT IS OVER. LEFT TO RIGHT: HENRY FORD II, CHARLES A.
LINDBERGH, THE AUTHOR, HENRY FORD, I. I. SIKORSKY.

mental Sikorsky undertaking. The project engineer, J. Russell Clark, rounded out the engineering representation. The chief mechanic, Adolph Plenefisch, and his assistant, J. Walker, were in charge of the ship. And the company photographer, Lew Oppel, took camera recordings of the event.

"The others?" he replied. "They were down on their knees in front of the ship. They were not praying—neither that the ship would fly, nor even that I would emerge unscathed from my experience. They were not praying at all. They were simply trying to get low enough to see if all four wheels were off the ground at the same time!"

Labensky, at least, had another thought in mind. The physique that had been built up in Russian naval training was still largely with him—and he was crouched low, arms outspread, muscles taut, ready to spring onto the craft and wrestle with it should it get out of control.

The VS-300 helicopter was the result of months of labor, years of planning that began away back in 1909, in Kiev, Russia. Sikorsky, a youth of twenty, had elected to enter aviation—a courageous choice at a time when aviation was frowned upon as a most unorthodox enterprise: a mild but dangerous form of insanity. But his family was imbued with no less courage than himself. His father and his sister risked not only their modest means to aid him in his ambition—they risked also reputation, which, for an eminent professor of psychology in a university town, was no light matter.

Sikorsky is characteristically thorough and fearless. His thoroughness led him at once to Paris to study the airplanes that were flying, or trying to fly, in this Mecca of aeronautics. His fearlessness led him to choose as his first project a totally different type of machine, one that others had practically discarded—the helicopter.

He returned to Kiev and began immediately to construct a flying model. It was a flimsy affair—crude, awkward. When it failed to fly, its creator rebuilt it, lopping off 100 pounds of its structural weight and increasing the diameter of its lifting rotors. With these changes the craft would raise its own weight, but other troubles immediately beset it. Stated briefly, it was both unstable and uncontrollable.[1]

Sikorsky, now twenty-one, made two mature decisions.

He decided, first, that the science of aeronautics had not reached the point where rotary-wing problems could be solved; and, second, that he himself needed considerable schooling in that science before he would be able to help overcome its deficiencies. So he put rotary wing in a cubbyhole and directed his attention toward the more conventional fixed-wing type of airplane.

His accomplishments in that field are a permanent part of aviation's history. His greatest contributions were in pioneering large aircraft: the first four-engined bombers, the first large cargo craft, the first transoceanic clippers—always the first, and almost always *big*.

But during all his success with *big* aircraft, he never forgot the helicopter in the cubbyhole. Every now and then he would tentatively withdraw it and look it over anew. The idea was like a tiny ember that would not die. When Cierva, the Spaniard, reached interesting results with the Autogiro, the ember glowed and Sikorsky's slide-rule worked overtime. He filed some underlying helicopter patents in 1930. When Germany's Dr. Focke publicized his FW-61 helicopter in 1937, Sikorsky lost little time in taking advantage of an opportunity to see it.

The ember was by now a flickering flame. It was uncertain still. It would need a tremendous amount of fuel to become a roaring fire—if he had known how much fuel, he might

[1] For interesting details of these early helicopter experiments, the reader is referred to Chaps. IV and V of "The Story of the Winged-S," by Igor I. Sikorsky.

have had reason to abandon it. But today, if you ask him how he succeeded in making a helicopter work when so many others had failed, he will say: "I do not know. Maybe it was just because nobody told me that it couldn't be done!"

That is not quite the truth. Many people did tell him. History itself proved it; and Sikorsky is a student of history and could not have escaped the warnings. Perhaps the confidence born of many successful accomplishments of the *impossible* spurred him on.

At any rate, during 1938, he developed his ideas. Early in 1939, he presented them to the officials of United Aircraft Corporation, of whose Vought-Sikorsky Division he was engineering manager, and a modest appropriation was voted to begin the project.

It was to be only a beginning. He was to build a simple, experimental framework on which he would mount an engine and a rotor,[1] to work out control and transmission problems. Further consideration would be given to extending the project after the initial work had been completed and evaluated. But it was the understanding of everyone, including Sikorsky, that the experimental framework would probably never leave the ground—or if, perchance, it should, it would simply be the forerunner of a more elaborate machine to be constructed after preliminary tests could be analyzed.

During the next four years, this *experimental framework* (or rather its aggregation of replaced cells) accumulated a total of more than 100 flying hours. It brought to this country the International Endurance Record for helicopters by remaining in the air for 1 hour, 32 minutes, 26.1 seconds. It formed the basis for a whole new series of helicopters of the Sikorsky type. And it stimulated interest throughout the nation to such an extent that, according to latest reports, there

[1] *Rotor* is the term applied to the *windmill* of an Autogiro or helicopter.

are upwards of sixty separate helicopter projects in all stages from artists' conceptions to actual flying craft.

And now, on October 7, 1943, it was scheduled to take its last curtain call at the entrance to the Edison Institute Museum. That morning, the engine was warmed up on the ramp at Ford Airport and I took off for the final "cross-country" flight—over a fence, a road, and two rows of trees to the front lawn of the institute. There the little silver craft awaited the arrival of the audience and the honored guests.

By one-thirty, Mr. and Mrs. Henry Ford were seated in the grandstand, surrounded by many top executives of the Ford Motor Company, as well as Mr. and Mrs. Charles A. Lindbergh and Mr. Sikorsky. A crowd estimated at several thousand persons lined the area that had been roped off for the helicopter's stage. It was less than 100 by 300 feet, surrounded by trees and with the museum building at one side; but it was ample space in which to perform all the VS-300's repertoire.

As the radio program began, I took off vertically, hovered in front of the grandstand, and the craft "bowed" to the guests. Then I backed off, stopped, and flew up to the stand again. After hovering a few seconds more, I swung around and flew down the little green strip, made a figure-eight below the tree-tops, and returned to where the mechanics, Al Krapish and Jimmie Maxwell, were standing, fifty feet apart. I nestled the nose of the ship in Krapish's upraised hand, then flew sideways and dropped it into Maxwell's—back and forth, sideways, from one to the other. After another figure-eight, I found that Krapish had laid a handkerchief on the ground in front of the grandstand, so I came to a stop directly above it, and slowly settled down until the left wheel rested in its very center.

A twelve-inch metal ring was set up on a pole, and I flew

over and plucked it off with the nose of the craft, sliding down sideways to deliver it to Krapish without landing. A few more pirouettes and a second landing on the handkerchief concluded my part of the demonstration.

Then Mr. Sikorsky stepped into the pilot's seat. He took off, hovered a while, and flew over to Krapish, who put a large bundle of postcards in the basket on the craft's nose—souvenirs to be carried by Mr. Sikorsky and the VS-300 on their last flight together. A couple of minutes later, he gently landed in front of the grandstand and turned off the switch.

The rotor whirred to a standstill. Mr. Sikorsky sat for a brief moment, then slowly climbed out and put his hand caressingly on the craft's silver nose. As I walked up, he said, "She was a good ship—a sweet little ship!"

I shared with him the feeling he expressed. We had taken our farewell of an aircraft that we both were going to miss.

Joseph Addison once wrote of the tombstones in Westminster Abbey: "Most of them recorded nothing else of the buried person, but that he was born upon one day, and died upon another; the whole history of his life being comprehended in those two circumstances that are common to all mankind."

In an effort to forestall such a fate for the VS-300 helicopter, the following pages contain the story of her life, her immediate successor, and a few comments about her possible influence on humanity.

## Chapter II

## THE VS-300 IS BORN

IN MAY, 1939, CHARLES H. GALE, EDITOR OF "SPORTSMAN Pilot," had arranged a private pilots' get-together in Washington, D. C., and as Commissioner of Aeronautics for Connecticut I happened to be a speaker on the same program as Mr. Sikorsky. After the luncheon and speeches, while I was talking with some friends, I found Mr. Sikorsky at my elbow, quietly waiting for me to notice him.

"Commissioner Morris," he said, with precise formality (he always employs the highest title applicable to an individual, and if he is not sure of the rank he makes it high enough to avoid offense), "if you could spare a minute when you are through, could I have a word with you?"

I acquiesced quickly, and we retired to a corner of the room, where he unfolded the story of his new, or renewed, interest—the helicopter. He spoke carefully at first, making a conscious effort to avoid enthusiasm as he emphasized that nothing had taken shape beyond very nebulous thinking.

"The ideas," he explained, "are only in the developmental stage, but I would be very pleased if you could drop down from Hartford some day and give me the benefit of your advice."

My advice!

What did I know about building airplanes that could be of the slightest help to one with Mr. Sikorsky's experience? And as for helicopters—well, I did tell him I had always felt that a helicopter was the answer to private flying. In fact, I had felt it so strongly that I had spent considerable time, a

8

year or two before, working on a flying model of one, and I let this drop in the course of the conversation. I am forever grateful to him that he didn't press for particulars. My *craft* was so utterly impossible, in the light of what I have since learned, that, had I given him details, I am sure it would have effectively queered any possibility of my ever becoming associated with his development.

However, at the mention of my confidence in the helicopter as a useful type of aircraft, his first wistfulness began to give way before the onslaught of overpowering enthusiasm for the project. He amplified many ideas of general design and vividly reviewed the potentialities of such a machine. His gray-blue eyes seemed almost black as they sparkled with enthusiasm and with hope.

"Of course," he concluded, "what I have told you must be held in the strictest confidence: the work is known to practically no one outside our own organization. But I would be pleased to have you as my guest if you could pay us a visit."

I arranged it within the next week or two, flew to Bridgeport, and was ushered into his office at the front of the engineering building. It was an interesting office, with photographs of his many successful craft on the walls, models on the table, bulging records in a bookcase, and chaos on the desk. But my eye was caught particularly by a display that occupied the position of honor in the center of his conference table. It was a metal framework supporting a three-foot section of a cherry tree that was about six inches in diameter. One end was sawed clean, but the other was torn and splintered as if struck by lightning.

"That is one of my favorite demonstrations," he explained with a smile. "One day in 1925 I was flying the S-29, the first Sikorsky airplane built in this country. I was delayed getting started for home, and en route I found myself caught by darkness. Not being entirely certain where I was, I decided to use the fading twilight to pick out a suitable spot for a landing. The small field that I chose—it was near Farmingdale, Long Island—had a few trees around it, but I thought I had judged the glide to miss them. I was in error: this cherry tree loomed out of the dusk and my wing struck it, snapping it off short. However, the ship continued on and the landing was successful.

"The following morning, inspection revealed that the basic wing structure was completely undamaged. So we put a patch of fabric over the gash in the leading edge, and I flew the ship home. I saved this sample of the tree to demonstrate the strength of my airplanes!"

Soon we settled into a discussion of the many helicopter problems he was trying to sort out in his mind. Should the control be by a conventional aircraft-type joy stick or by a wheel? Would it be satisfactory to operate the rudder by a steering wheel instead of by the usual rudder pedals? Should the lift be controlled by a lever beside the pilot, and if so, on which side? These and many other questions he laid before me, and I fear my total ignorance of helicopter design details must have been all too apparent in my inconclusive answers.

At one point he sought to clarify the fundamental principles for me. From the wealth of confusion atop his desk, he unearthed a toy similar to one I used to play with as a boy. It was a flat piece of metal, twisted so that it formed a kind of long screw-thread; and fitted over it was a tin propeller blade with a slot at the center.

"If I may disturb you for a moment," he said, "I would like to show you how this works."

He led me outside his office and slipped the propeller over the twisted rod. "Now, when I slide the propeller off the rod, it will turn at a very high speed and will fly—like this," and he gave a mighty pull. It did. It flew halfway down the drafting room, and the men at the boards glanced up with amazement, amusement, and even disdain variously registered on their faces. He retrieved it and prepared to repeat the experiment.

"That time," he explained, "I tilted the rod so that the propeller had considerable horizontal motion. That is why it landed so far away. But it will fly straight up if I hold the rod vertically." He sent it off again with a zing, and after several seconds among the rafters directly overhead, it settled back into his hands.

He concluded the demonstration by interpreting the principles that were successfully employed in the toy and explaining how these principles could lead to similar success in a full-fledged helicopter.

What he may have gained from my visit I never discovered. What I gained was a growing conviction that I wanted nothing more in this world than to become associated with his project. The weeks passed, and I could no longer hold my peace. In late June, I called him to see if I might drop down again, and the usual welcome was extended.

"Mr. Sikorsky," I said across the luncheon table, "as Commissioner of Aeronautics I have a definite official interest in your helicopter development. Connecticut is fortunate and proud to count you among her citizens and business leaders."

"Thank you very much, Commissioner Morris," he said with a low bow that emphasized his continental courtesy.

"But," I continued, taking advantage of the wedge I had just driven, "I have a very real *personal* interest in your work, as well. I would not care to stay in my present position forever, even if I could survive the vagaries of politics—of which there is some doubt. So I have spent the last several years watching for an opening in aviation that seemed to offer a sound future. I am convinced that your helicopter has that future, and I would be extremely grateful if you would be willing to consider this conversation as my application for employment in any position for which I may be qualified."

In his polite manner, he asked if he might take the matter under advisement, and he did it in such a way as to make me feel I had bestowed a great honor upon him by even thinking of the idea. Then the conversation turned to other topics, and he asked me which one of the smaller aircraft engines I preferred. I unhesitatingly stated my choice, and told him that the ship I had flown down for this very meeting was powered with an engine of that make.

He showed unusual interest, I thought, for a man whose major endeavors had always been in the realm of large, multi-engined airplanes with several thousand horsepower. As he talked, he was working something over in his mind, and finally he came out with it. "Would it be possible for me to have a ride in your ship?"

Within five minutes we were back at the airport, and the 110 horses in the nose of the little biplane were champing at the throttle. We flew around for fifteen or twenty minutes while my passenger handled the controls and studied the response of the engine.

I didn't know at the time that this flight would be at least one of the factors that resulted in the decision to use this same type of engine in the first Army experimental helicopter. And I certainly had not the slightest notion that I would be the test pilot in that craft.

After we landed, the airport manager called me to one side. "Holy smoke, Les," he said, "why didn't you tell us you were going to take Sikorsky up in that little crate? We would

have had a batch of cameras here. Why, he never flies in anything but the big clippers!"

I have always regretted that my association with the helicopter did not mature until 1941, so that I missed a year and
a half of first-hand contact with its earliest development. By
September, 1939, extensive ground trials of the fundamental
mechanisms had been concluded, and the crude, experimental
VS-300 was ready for its initial attempts at flight. The "VS"
stood for Vought-Sikorsky, the division of United Aircraft
Corporation of which Mr. Sikorsky was engineering manager. The "300" was the company model number assigned to
this elementary framework of exposed tubes and struts. The
pilot perched on a tiny seat in the open air in front of the
seventy-five-horsepower engine, surrounded by nothing but
imagination and supported by little more than hope. A long,
boxlike structure of riveted sheet metal extended rearward
and supported the single-bladed tail rotor. From the engine
shaft, five V belts carried the power upward to a large pulley
just outside a transmission box that contained gears from the
rear end of a heavy-duty truck. Above the transmission was
a short, stubby shaft on which was mounted the heart of the
machine—the main rotor hub and blades.

The landing gear had four widespread wheels—two at the
sides, one under the nose, and one toward the tail. In order
to eliminate as many sources of potential trouble as possible,
the wheels were so mounted that they could swivel in any
direction. If the pilot should land sideways, for instance, the
wheels would turn and he would roll as readily as he would
fore and aft.

On September 14, the ship was taken to an unused portion
of the factory yard and was made ready for her sink-or-swim
trials. Mr. Sikorsky, with tense eagerness, carefully inspected

the last-minute arrangements. Finally, he stepped into the open seat and drew the safety belt around him.

His mind flashed back momentarily to a time, almost thirty years earlier, when he had left the ground in an airplane for the first time. He was testing his first ship in Russia, in 1910: he had never flown before; he had never had any flight instruction; and he didn't even know whether the craft was capable of getting into the air, much less whether it would be controllable if it did. The results of his first flight, dubious at the time but eminently successful in the light of later events, must have strengthened him for his present job.

He glanced at the moorings of the little helicopter. At each wheel a sturdy rope was attached with only a few inches of slack, lest Nature should take a stronger course than man was prepared to follow.

He started the engine, and the ship vibrated badly and rocked like an angry elephant at his pickets. The controls shook in the pilot's hand. He bounced and swayed in the seat. Then he slowly began to apply power, and the frail structure shivered more violently. Finally he had a feeling that she might be ready to take off. He came up a little more on the pitch control, and the craft lifted to the point where one or two wheels were momentarily free of the ground. Another application of power, and there was little doubt that she was in the air.

But both she and her pilot were so new and inexperienced that it was only a momentary hop. He dropped the pitch almost instantly and settled back to a more comfortable rocking at slower idling speeds, while he conferred with his associates.

Again he went through the preliminary approaches to flight, and this time, after a little more power and a great deal more shaking, he pulled all four wheels off the ground. Just for an instant! Then down on the pitch again.

A few brief *flights*, totaling perhaps ten seconds in the air, concluded the first day of life for the VS-300.

Her existence from then on was destined to be very hectic, and the next few weeks were no exception. She was tried, changed, and tried again. Time after time a new adjustment was made, or a new installation worked out. Sometimes it was kept; more often it became just another discarded idea.

In November, flights began in earnest, and quite often they lasted for several minutes at a time. There were two pilots by now—Serge Gluhareff, executive engineer and pilot in his own right, had joined in this part of the work. He and Mr. Sikorsky took turns at the controls and compared notes on their findings. The earlier mooring cables had been done away with, and in their place a heavy weight was suspended below the ship to prevent it from rising more than a few feet. The weight would drag back and forth over the ground as the pilots carefully tried to move forward, backward, or sideways.

Adolph Plenefisch, crew chief in those early days and now foreman-at-large on the experimental program, recalls this period with a mixture of pleasure and resentment.

"If you could have only seen us!" he says. "Every time they would start down the ramp, we would run after them. Then they'd stop and back up, and we'd run the other way. Back and forth, back and forth, until our tongues were hanging out a mile. But we could see that she was flying better every day. So we didn't care. We were proud of her. You should have heard the ragging we took, though. The other fellows in the shop couldn't see the purpose in it all. 'Igor's nightmare,' they called it. Oh, they used to kid us something awful!"

However, the shop men were not the only ones to snicker. One of the most capable engineers in the organization was heard to say, "If that thing ever flies, I have never been, am not, and never will be an engineer." The ship *did* fly—and he didn't lose his professional reputation as a result of that rash remark. But his comment expressed the skepticism that widely attended the growing pains of the VS-300. She was considered, both by informed people and by the public at large, a freak child, awkward, with no hope of fulfilling a purpose in life. She was an outcast, admired by none but her own closest family.

Day by day she developed. Slowly ideas began to crystallize. Progress was being made. Then on December 9, 1939, the first accident to befall a Sikorsky helicopter overtook her. Gluhareff was at the controls and was landing close to the buildings under very gusty conditions. All at once a blast of wind whipped around the corner and started him drifting sideways. He settled to the ground, and, in the twinkling of an eye, the craft was over on her side, grinding off the rotor blades on the pavement. The pilot himself was unhurt. The craft, of course, suffered major injuries.

This gave an opportunity for extensive reconsideration. A careful review was made of all points in the record to date. The successes were analyzed and given their proper weight in the discussion. The shortcomings were brought out for a thorough airing, and looming largest among them was the major bugbear of all earlier helicopters—*control.* Control seemed to be only just sufficient, and it was very tricky and delicate—as evidenced by the results of the last flight.

So it was decided that *cyclical-pitch* [1] control would be abandoned, at least for the time being. In its place, two extra control propellers would be provided at the tail of the craft. They would be mounted in a horizontal plane, one at each side of the ship, so that an increase in their pitch (or *bite*) would raise the tail and a decrease in their pitch would lower

[1] This is one name for the type of control that was used up to that time. A fuller explanation is given later in the book.

it. Then, of course, it was necessary to control sideways
*rolling*—and this would be accomplished by an increase in the
pitch of one tail propeller, making it raise that side of the
ship, while at the same time decreasing the pitch of the other
one so that it would lower that side.

On March 6, 1940, the craft was back in the air again. The
new controls, though uglier, were much more satisfactory,
and after a moderate amount of self-teaching, the pilots could
handle the ship accurately and effectively. Bit by bit, the re-
strictive cables were eased off. Soon, extended flights were
made with the cables slack, and with men holding them just
in case anything undesirable should develop.

During the spring of 1940, controlled flights became the
rule, instead of the exception. Every good day found the ship
in the air, undergoing composite tests and pilot training. At
last the remaining semblance of restraint was cast aside, the
cables were removed, and on May 13, Mr. Sikorsky left the
ground for the first free flight in the VS-300.

Now seemed the time for this still awkward child to make
her debut to the public. On May 20, the invited guests gathered at Bridgeport Airport. I was privileged to be among
them, and this was my first opportunity to see an actual flight,
although I had been following her progress closely.

It was interesting to note the questions that were asked as
the visitors inspected the craft before the flight. Mr. Sikorsky
was pressed into a detailed explanation of the controls, and
his listeners were surprised to learn how fundamentally simple the principles were. Like many other startling inventions,
the idea, once thought out and reduced to practice, makes
you feel like saying, "Why, of course! Why didn't anyone
do this before?" Many people had tried—but it required a
touch of genius to achieve success.

Perhaps the most general, if guarded, comment pertained
to the craft's appearance. No fancy streamlining here! Every

detail was a vital, integral part, without which the craft simply would not function. There was no chrome plating, no
decorations, no extras whatsoever; just a plain, exposed framework of steel tubes supporting an unconcealed engine, a bare
drive shaft, and a hundred little bits and pieces of control rods
and cables that somehow worked together to accomplish an
amazing result.

Mr. Sikorsky explained, without apology, that no thought
had been given to making the craft beautiful. "There will be

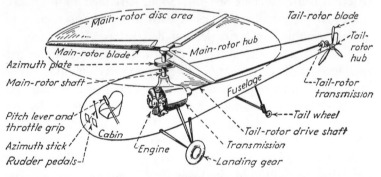

GENERAL ARRANGEMENT OF SIKORSKY-TYPE HELICOPTER (MAJOR COM-
PONENTS ONLY).

plenty of time for that," he said. "Until now, and for some
time to come, we shall be developing principles, not details.
Once we have achieved our primary objectives, we may perhaps try to dress it up a little."

In reality, that was only a part of the story. Mr. Sikorsky
has always believed in keeping his creative genius as free as
possible. He knew that the greatest strides would be made if
a change, even a major one, could be instituted overnight by
means of a hack saw and a welding torch, without regret at
spoiling a superficial appearance. That same reasoning was
largely responsible for the use of V belts to transmit the
VS-300's power: alterations were much more readily accomplished than would have been the case with inflexible shafts

THE TEST STAND THAT GAVE BASIC INFORMATION FOR THE VS-300. ITS SHAFT
WAS THE REAR AXLE OF AN AUTOMOBILE. THE TRANSMISSION WAS THE AUTO-
MOBILE'S DIFFERENTIAL. V BELTS CARRIED THE POWER FROM A MOTORCYCLE
ENGINE TO THE SINGLE-BLADED ROTOR.

MR. SIKORSKY POSES BY THE VS-300 JUST BEFORE MAKING THE FIRST FLIGHTS ON SEPTEMBER 14, 1939.

QUARTERING REAR VIEW OF VS-300, AS FIRST FLOWN.

BY NOVEMBER, 1939, SHORT "CAPTIVE" FLIGHTS (NOTE THE BALL AND CHAIN) WERE BECOMING REGULAR PROCEDURE. SERGE GLUHAREFF AS PILOT.

REBUILT AFTER ITS FIRST ACCIDENT, THE VS-300, MINUS THE MAIN ROTOR, WAS MOUNTED ON A SWIVELING SUPPORT SO THE PILOTS (MR. SIKORSKY IN THIS PICTURE) COULD TRAIN THEMSELVES.

MR. SIKORSKY MAKES SOME EXTENDED FLIGHTS WITH ROPES ATTACHED IN CASE OF UNFORESEEN DEVELOPMENTS. HIS LEFT HAND IS ON THE MAIN PITCH LEVER WHICH CONTROLS HEIGHT ABOVE THE GROUND. HIS RIGHT HAND OPERATES THE STICK TO HOLD THE CRAFT LEVEL, BOTH SIDEWAYS AND FORE-AND-AFT.

and gears. Once the mechanical or structural details should become fixed, the development would, at least in a measure, be fettered thereafter to the pre-established form.

When the guests had completed their inspection and had received answers to their myriad questions, Mr. Sikorsky perched himself in the pilot's seat. The engine purred, the rotor blades whirled around, and the cameras clicked. He took off straight up for a few feet, then hung there, and, like a king on his dais benevolently looking out upon his subjects after some good deed, Mr. Sikorsky surveyed brightly the crowd of upturned faces. Pleased and encouraged by the astonishment he saw there, he proceeded to show how the little craft would fly backward, go sideways, straight up or straight down, and even turn around on a spot.

He didn't fly forward very much. I discovered a year later, when I began to try my hand at this same craft, that forward flight was not too satisfactory—in fact, it was quite uncertain! During this period in the craft's development, Mr. E. E. Wilson, at that time President of the corporation, in one of his discussions with Mr. Sikorsky, said, "I have seen the moving pictures of the helicopter hovering over a spot, rising straight up, settling straight down, flying sideways and even backward—all under excellent control. But I haven't seen any films of it flying forward." To which Mr. Sikorsky replied, "Mr. Wilson, that is one of the minor engineering problems that we haven't yet solved!"

However, for this particular demonstration, forward flight was not required. Everyone assumed that an aircraft that could do all those other things must certainly be able to fly forward. So the debut was a grand success.

In my pocket I had been carrying a little slip of paper as a surprise for Mr. Sikorsky. He had once dropped a cautious hint that he would be extremely pleased if the first helicopter pilot license could be issued in his name. Our state laws provided for the issuance of special licenses, and since he had no wish to apply for one of the regular classifications, it was entirely proper to give him a special *helicopter* rating.

After the demonstration was over, I stepped up to him and delivered the envelope.

"Mr. Sikorsky," I said, "now that you have satisfactorily demonstrated to me your ability to fly the helicopter, I am happy to present you with Connecticut Helicopter Pilot License No. 1."

# Chapter III

## *ADOLESCENCE*

T HE YEAR 1940 WAS ADOLESCENCE TO THE VS-300. SHE
was going through the most important and critical
stage in her career. Work progressed haltingly because
the engineers had to feel their way laboriously through each
trouble that beset her. Unlike many other fields of endeavor,
experience could not be hired—it had to be developed on
the spot.

By July, a ninety-horsepower engine was installed to give
a little margin of power, and flights as long as twenty-five
minutes were recorded. Other changes in the ship made it
possible to fly forward at moderate speeds up to thirty or
forty miles an hour, although occasionally some mysterious,
uncontrollable antics would warn that operations were on
the fringe of hidden danger. The pilots were rounding out
their training, and toward the end of the summer a large
number of flights were made to register in moving pictures
the gains that had been made.

One morning my phone rang. "Sikorsky speaking," came
the slow, courteous voice at the other end. "We are planning
to fly quite extensively today, and if you would care to come
down we should be delighted to have you with us."

I hopped into our ship and, as I circled Bridgeport Airport, I saw the little craft already in the air. Movies were
plentifully taken—movies of the helicopter doing all its usual
tricks and many new ones. They included a demonstration
of Mr. Sikorsky flying up to Michael Gluhareff standing on
a pile of rocks. While the ship hovered there, Gluhareff

21

placed a suitcase in a wire basket attached to the fuselage; then Mr. Sikorsky backed away and flew off with his load. He returned shortly, and the suitcase was removed, all without a landing being made. This scene was repeated several times to emphasize the craft's control, both vertically and horizontally. The entire, underlying *raison d'être* of the helicopter is exemplified by its ability to stop at a spot, remain virtually motionless for a period of time, and then *back* away.

One section of the film taken on this day was never released to the public, but it can now be told, without jeopardizing the helicopter's future, that on one of the trials Mr. Sikorsky didn't quite stop in time. With gentle insistence, Gluhareff was nudged down from his rocky perch!

Toward the end of the afternoon, Mr. Sikorsky electrified everyone by announcing that he was about to make the first American "cross-country" helicopter flight. We were all aghast at the idea—until he outlined his route.

"We shall push the ship," he explained, "down the road toward the factory. Then I will take off crosswise of the road —something that no other aircraft can do—and fly over that cabbage patch to the airport."

As we surveyed the area, we had to admit that, except for a large ditch beside the airport runway, there were no hazards. The total distance was probably 250 yards, and the machine had often flown much farther than this continuously over the airport. The cameras were set up, the craft was placed at the proper spot, and the engine was started for this epochal event!

Mr. Sikorsky pulled up on the pitch-control lever, and the VS-300 took off vertically from the road. The pilot hovered for a few seconds, then dipped the nose and began to gain speed until he was moving about twenty-five miles an hour, fifteen feet above the cabbages. As we look back on it now, we realize that the flight included several fits and a couple of starts, but it was a genuine thrill to think that we were witnessing the first cross-country flight of a helicopter in the Western Hemisphere—a flight that had begun at one point and was wending its way toward another given point.

The tall cattails by the ditch at the edge of the airport bowed low as the craft went by. The flight was almost completed. Mr. Sikorsky eased back on the stick and had practically stopped over the runway when something went wrong. We could see the entire structure suddenly begin a violent shaking, fifteen feet in the air, and it was obvious that control was gone. The ship rolled viciously to one side, then to the other, then began to turn as it sank rapidly toward the ground. It struck hard, still right side up, bounced once, rolled a few feet, and ended up heading in the direction from which it had come.

When we reached the scene, Mr. Sikorsky was standing calmly beside the ship, studying the main rotor hub. He was chewing his cheek, as he so often does when he is deep in thought. Finally he asked Plenefisch to check the condition of the oil dampers—the hydraulic pistons and cylinders that were mounted above the rotor blades to prevent undesirable vibrations.

Plenefisch reported that they were without oil. Some time previously, it had been questioned whether they were really required, and the crew had been instructed not to refill them. In this way, their necessity would be investigated. It so happened that, until now, no forces had been encountered that would excite the natural frequencies of the rotor. This particular flight, however, proved that under some circumstances, damping could not be dispensed with—and another lesson was learned by experience.

Some weeks later, after many more successful flying days, Mr. Sikorsky was testing the craft in forward flight to analyze the troubles that began at speeds of thirty to forty miles an hour. As he was making a run about twenty feet above the ground, one of the tail outriggers gave way and folded upward, slacking off on the rubber belts that drove the horizontal rotor. That rotor slowed down immediately, while the one on the other side continued to turn at normal speed. With the resultant loss of control, the craft rolled over in the air and fell sideways in a tangled mass of wreckage.

One of the mechanics who was there at the time reports that Mr. Sikorsky extricated himself from the debris and stood for a long minute looking it all over. Then he said in quiet finality, "I think we will get her home now."

The cause of this accident was found to be an old crack, presumably traceable to the earlier severe landing at the end of the "first cross-country flight."

This turbulent period of troubles and successes, hodgepodged together, was marked by another development of signal importance.

At a meeting in Philadelphia, Mr. Sikorsky had become acquainted with Lieut. H. F. Gregory of the Army Air Forces, who was actively engaged in the Army's rotary-wing developmental program. This program had been primarily concerned, until then, with Autogiro projects; but in its broad aspects it covered anything with a rotor on top, and this included the helicopter.

At Mr. Sikorsky's invitation, Gregory and an associate, Lieut. V. R. Haugen, visited Bridgeport to investigate the work that was going on there. I dropped in for the day, and thus was on hand when they were accorded the opportunity of actually flying the VS-300.

Gregory stepped in first. The ship was designed to carry only one person, so Mr. Sikorsky could not ride with him while giving initial training. Instead, he stood beside the open nose section while Gregory felt out the controls and listened carefully to the words of instruction.

"I think you will find," said Mr. Sikorsky, "that she has quite sensitive lateral control. She will want to rock sharply to left and right. If you will not try to control her too much, you may find it better."

"This lever," he continued, "is the main pitch control. Pull it up, to leave the ground. When you want to land, push it slightly down again; but if things are unsatisfactory in any way, do not hesitate to push it down abruptly. You may, perhaps, land a little hard, but you will be firmly anchored to the ground because all lift will be gone from the rotor."

Explanations completed, Mr. Sikorsky stepped aside and left Gregory to develop his own solutions from that point onward. He tried the throttle once or twice, then set it at the predetermined point. Holding the control stick neutral with his right hand, he began to pull upward on the pitch-control lever with his left. The rotor speeded up, and gradually the machine became lighter. As the wheels left the ground, it was readily apparent that Mr. Sikorsky's warning about sensitive lateral control might as well never have been given. The craft rocked briskly from side to side, and after a few seconds Gregory pushed down on the pitch control and landed with a sheepish grin on his face. He tried it a second time, and smoothed it out somewhat. After the third or fourth brief attempt he began to learn the trick and was able to hover continuously, albeit without the perfection that Mr. Sikorsky had gained or that he himself developed later.

Then he undertook to try moving sideways and backward slightly. Bit by bit, the ship came under his control.

Finally, he decided to attempt some forward flights. All went well for a time; but when he was moving at about ten miles an hour, the craft began to climb away from the ground and we could see Gregory concentrating furiously to get her down again. He lowered the pitch control too much, and she settled too fast. He pulled up on it too hard, and she **began** to float upward. She bobbed around like a toy balloon in a gale. But he finally succeeded in making a nice landing and sat there grinning again and shaking his head in relief.

"I thought I had everything in hand," he explained, "but that extra lift when she started forward fooled me."

"Yes," said Mr. Sikorsky. "Perhaps I should have warned you about that. After the ship has made the transition from hovering to forward flight, there is a surplus of power and you have to drop off considerably on the pitch-control lever or you will climb quite rapidly."

"So I found!" Gregory chuckled. "I thought for a minute that I was going to set an altitude record. May I take another try at it?"

Mr. Sikorsky agreed, and Gregory spent ten minutes more rounding out his experience. By the end of that time, we could see that his troubles were over and the ship was obeying his commands.

Haugen was next and went through pretty much the same routine that Gregory had—overcontrol at the beginning, with the attendant rocking from side to side; then the difficulty with forward flight. But he, like Gregory, mastered it in short order, and when he was through, Mr. Sikorsky extended his congratulations to them both and warmly welcomed them to the exclusive ranks of helicopter pilots.

Then began a friendly discussion that has carried over even to the present time. It pertained to the pronunciation of the word *helicopter*. Mr. Sikorsky used a long *e*—"heel-i-copter." He liked to call his ship the *heely* (spelled heli), and it would have bordered on the profane with a short *e* as in "hell." Gregory maintained that the short *e* was correct, and subsequent reference to Webster and other sources supported his contention. The word stems from the Greek *helix*, meaning "spiral," and *pteron*, meaning "wing."

Lexicographers can correctly point out that all derivatives

from *helix* use the short *e* (helical, helicoid, etc.); those from *helios*, meaning "sun," are long (heliotrope, heliometer, heliocentric, etc.). Nevertheless, the fact remains that those experts, including even Mr. Webster, never produced a *hell*-icopter that would work, whereas Mr. Sikorsky has made a very successful *heel*-icopter. If this argument is not sufficiently convincing, it is submitted that the public itself will not long endure a four-syllable word with four short vowels. Therefore, if lexicographers' rules refuse to recognize inventive genius, perhaps common usage may sometime settle the problem.

Gregory's interest in the Sikorsky helicopter was more than curiosity. Congress had recently appropriated $3,000,000 for the Army to develop rotary-wing aircraft, and Gregory was the project officer in charge. As a result of his visit, Mr. Sikorsky went to work on a design for the VS-316 Helicopter, Two-place Observation Trainer, and United Aircraft submitted its proposal to the Army. Although Sikorsky Aircraft had pioneered in the helicopter field, the first Army contract went to another company. It was only a short time after this, however, that Sikorsky Aircraft was given a separate contract for the construction of one helicopter.

Thus, 1940 saw the Sikorsky helicopter program emerge from behind the closed door of research and take on an uncertain status in the public eye. The VS-300 had proved many points, but it still left much to be desired both in appearance and in performance. There had been a couple of accidents, but fortunately no one had suffered so much as a scratch. And the Army had shown interest enough in the idea to contract for one of the craft.

*Chapter IV*

## ON THE PAST IS BUILT THE FUTURE

ONE AFTERNOON IN JANUARY, 1941, I RECEIVED ANOTHER telephone call from Mr. Sikorsky.

"Commissioner Morris," he said, "along the lines of our previous discussions, would you be interested in joining our organization as a test pilot on the helicopter?"

My heart leaped as he hastened apologetically to explain: "I would not expect you to make any flights that I myself would be unwilling to make. But, as you know, we are working on this Army contract, and the pressure of my other duties will make it increasingly difficult for me to give as much time to test flying as it will require."

No apologies were necessary. What other spot in the aircraft industry could offer so much of interest—so much for the future—as to be a test pilot of the helicopter? Without hesitation, I accepted over the telephone, and on March 17, I arrived at Stratford, prepared to go to work.

The first two months were spent in learning all I could about the helicopter—past, present, and future—and I was astonished at the dearth of reference data of a type that I was able to understand.

"Prof" Sikorsky came to my rescue. Prof, a relative of Mr. Sikorsky's, sits, day after day, with a slide-rule half the size of his desk and makes sense out of an intricate complexity of formulas and figures. I shall never forget the time he asked me if I would check over a 260-page report that he had prepared. In my innocence, I accepted the assignment. Page after page of mathematical integrals and calculations met my gaze as I thumbed the book and grew Lilliputian in my own esteem. Then I stumbled on three lines of type that were written in the English language, and I was relieved to find that this was the conclusion to be drawn from the preceding thirty-seven pages of mystery. The conclusion was interesting and, for all I could tell, correct—so I hastily thumbed further. Twenty-three pages later, I discovered another conclusion; and by the end of the report I had unearthed enough so that, if they had all been lumped together and double-spaced, they might have filled one page. The other 259 pages were substantiation!

DA VINCI'S CONCEPTION.

Discouraged, I returned the report to Prof and confessed my inabilities. He was very charitable and showed me his private stock of reference material. He took considerable time discussing the contents of each pamphlet and recommending certain ones for basic data. I retired with three or four that offered promise of being readable, and almost at once, my eyes were opened.[1]

I found, for instance, that the basic concept of the helicopter really goes back as far as Leonardo da Vinci who, toward the end of the fifteenth century, sketched a crude craft of this type. He proposed using a screw-thread on a vertical shaft, believing correctly that if it were large enough, properly designed, and properly powered it would draw itself into the air. As with so many of da Vinci's ideas, civilization took four centuries to complete the job.

[1] It is not the author's purpose to report here all early helicopter projects. Those that are mentioned are chosen primarily to emphasize the antiquity of the idea and the many different approaches that have been tried.

In 1784 two Frenchmen, Launoy and Bienvenu, constructed a simple scientific toy helicopter with feathers for
blades. This was the great-great-grandfather of the toy with
which Mr. Sikorsky demonstrated helicopter principles that
day in his office. The French device used a bent bow for
motive power.

Da Vinci's sketch and the Frenchmen's toy indicate the
trend of the many helicopter proposals that died, before ma-

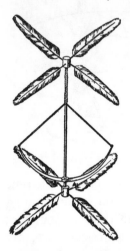

turing, in the pre-gasoline-engine era.
However, in 1907, two separate projects appeared in France. One was
sponsored by Paul Cornu and one by
Louis Breguet—a name famous in airplane history. Cornu's craft had a
twenty-four-horsepower engine and
two main rotors. The reason for having two of them was to neutralize
engine torque. If you stand on ice,
with a long board across your shoulders, and try to make the board turn
quickly, you will find that quite the
opposite occurs. Instead of your turn-

LAUNOY-BIENVENU TOY.   ing the board, the board turns you.

The same is true of a helicopter. If
you have only one rotor, driven by an engine in the fuselage,
the rotor turns one way, but the fuselage wants to turn the
other. This is the result of engine torque.

Cornu planned to neutralize this torque by having two rotors turning in opposite directions. From an engineering point
of view the scheme is sound and has been applied in a major-
ity of helicopter projects. For control, he hung vanes in the
air stream, or down-wash, below the rotors, expecting to
guide the machine by tilting the vanes. Actually, the speed of
the down-wash isn't very great, and Cornu's venture came to

grief because of the same two factors that were destined to cause a large number of helicopter failures: lack of control and lack of stability. However, he deserves a permanent niche in history because his craft developed enough lift to raise itself from the ground, and it was the first full-scale helicopter to show signs of success.

The other French helicopter, contemporary with Cornu's, was the first one designed by Breguet. This machine had four main rotors and was able to reach a height of four feet. It was barely controllable, however, and was quite unsteady in the air.

In the autumn of the following year, 1908, a nineteen-year-old Russian boy was vacationing with his father in Berlin. He heard authenticated reports of the Wright brothers' flights and was instantly so fired with enthusiasm that he spent his vacation building a large-scale model of a helicopter and working out the details in his hotel room.

His sincerity was so apparent to his father that the young man found himself headed for Paris with sufficient funds to purchase an aircraft engine, enroll in an aviation school, and remain for five months absorbing information from the many pioneers who were using Paris as their headquarters. This gave him the opportunity to crystallize his ideas in his own mind before returning to Kiev to put them into practice. During this time, he journeyed to Lisieux, 100 miles west of Paris, and spent a day with Cornu looking over his helicopter. He didn't see it operate, but he accumulated many thoughts for the time he would be building his own craft.

In the spring he returned to Kiev, and within a few months his helicopter was finished. The young man was Igor Sikorsky. The machine he had constructed had a twenty-five-horsepower Anzani engine bought in Paris; and it utilized two main rotors, mounted one above the other on concentric shafts. To save many words in future explanations, it appears

## VARIOUS BASIC CONFIGURATIONS OF THE HELICOPTER

### TWIN ROTOR
Two main rotors turning in opposite directions
("contra-rotating") to neutralize torque

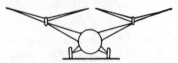

COAXIAL (both rotors mounted on the same axle); the usual type in early experiments

BIAXIAL- Having two axles on lateral out-riggers. This is the type of the German FW-61 and the American Platt-Le Page. Another biaxial arrangement is shown below, with blades overlapping and meshing like an egg-beater

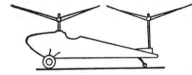

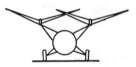

BIAXIAL- Longitudinally disposed

BIAXIAL-Meshing

### SINGLE MAIN ROTOR
One rotor for lift, with means for torque compensation

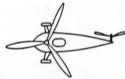

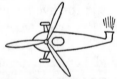

Torque compensated by a tail rotor. This is the Von Baumhauer and Sikorsky type

Torque compensated by a tail jet (blower or explosive mixture)

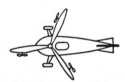

Torque eliminated by driving the rotor with propellers mounted on the blades

Torque eliminated by driving the rotor with jets in the blades

advisable to introduce here two terms that may sound technical but really are not—*contra-rotating*, meaning "turning in opposite directions," and *coaxial*, meaning "having the same axis or axle." Thus, Sikorsky's first helicopter rotors were contra-rotating and coaxial. Vanes, hung below the rotors as in the Cornu ship, were intended to supply control.

This first machine was unable to lift its own weight from the ground. So, during the winter, it was rebuilt to make it 100 pounds lighter and to increase the diameter of the rotors. When trials were resumed in the spring, the craft could rise in the air, but it was beset by the basic helicopter illnesses of insufficient control and stability.

So, as stated in an earlier chapter, Sikorsky decided that his knowledge of aviation was not at the stage where he could solve helicopter problems. He turned his attention to other projects, and during the next thirty years, his name became famous because of his success with large airplanes. But throughout it all, his mind kept returning periodically to the helicopter for review and further analysis.

In the interim, others were also busy with this type of craft. In 1916, for example, two Austrians, Petroczy and von Kármán, developed a craft with three 120-horsepower engines and coaxial contra-rotating rotors. Their craft was designed for observation, not for transportation. It was always held by cables and, so far as is known, it never carried human cargo. Nevertheless, several captive flights were made at respectable altitudes, with the duration ranging up to as much as one hour.

The early 1920's were rife with rotary-wing development. Perhaps the most outstanding achievement was the Autogiro, designed in Spain and in large measure perfected in England by Juan de la Cierva. Cierva first considered building a helicopter, but he stumbled on a most interesting phenomenon that completely altered his approach. Musing on the fact that an airplane wing in a glide has not only upward lift but also forward pull, he wondered what would happen if a wing should be held at one end so that it would keep turning in a circle. He experimented with the idea and worked out the fundamentals of *autorotation*—that phenomenon which keeps the Autogiro rotor whirling at all times in flight, without benefit of engine power.

This is the basic difference between the Autogiro and the helicopter. The helicopter's engine is geared directly to its

THE PETROCZY-VON KÁRMÁN.

rotor; hence, it is often called a *direct-lift* aircraft. The Autogiro, on the other hand, is pulled (or sometimes pushed) through the air by a conventional propeller. Its rotor is not driven by the engine, except for starting on the ground. Once in flight, it continues to turn due to the action of the air on the blades, and therefore it must keep moving through the air. If it ceases to move forward, it must settle, which explains why the Autogiro is incapable of true *hovering*.

About the same time that Cierva was starting his experiments, a number of helicopter developments were under way in various parts of the world. Notable among them were the projects of Henry A. Berliner and of Georges de Bothezat in

A RECENT AUTOGIRO (NOTE PROPELLER IN THE NOSE).

THE AUTHOR (THEN COMMISSIONER OF AERONAUTICS FOR CONNECTICUT) PRE-
SENTS MR. SIKORSKY WITH HELICOPTER PILOT LICENSE NO. 1 (SEE P. 20).

THE FIRST HELICOPTER PICKUP—MICHAEL GLUHAREFF TO MR. SIKORSKY (SEE
P. 21).

MR. SIKORSKY MAKES A HIGH FLIGHT WITH THE EARLY OUTRIGGER CONTROLS.

VARIOUS SHAPES AND SIZES OF TAIL OUTRIGGERS WERE TRIED DURING 1940 AND 1941, IN AN EFFORT TO OVERCOME CONTROL PROBLEMS.

the United States, Etienne Œhmichen in France, and Marquis Pateras Pescara in Spain.

FIRST BERLINER.

SECOND BERLINER.

Berliner built two entirely different ships between 1920 and 1923. The first was the then popular twin-rotor coaxial type, and the second had two rotors mounted on outriggers, one on each side of the fuselage. Both arrangements proved unstable, but there was sufficient control for flights of several minutes' duration. An eighty-horsepower engine was used.

De Bothezat built his ship around a 200-horsepower engine and used four sizable rotors mounted at the ends of a cross-shaped fuselage structure. Two small auxiliary propellers, turning in a vertical plane, provided rudder control. The craft was complicated, but moderately stable and controlla-

THE DE BOTHEZAT.

ble. It made numerous flights, all of short duration and not far off the ground. His work was conducted at the Army's McCook Field in Dayton, and several of his collaborators are still at Wright Field, either as officers or civilians, associated with current Army helicopter projects.

Œhmichen, in France, tackled the problem from a compromise angle. His first craft had a gas-filled balloon to furnish part of the lift. His second had four main rotors, five auxiliary horizontal propellers [1] for control, a vertical propeller for steering, and two conventional propellers to provide forward speed. A 120-horsepower engine was used in this craft, and it is amazing that, with such a complex mecha-

---

[1] The term *horizontal propeller*, as used in this book, means a propeller whose plane of rotation is horizontal. Thus a *horizontal propeller* is mounted on a *vertical* shaft; and a *vertical propeller* is mounted on a *horizontal* shaft.

nism, involving thirteen separate transmission systems, the craft was able to make over one thousand flights, many of which were of several minutes' duration.

THE ŒHMICHEN.

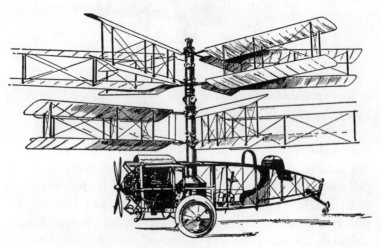

THE PESCARA.

Pescara's efforts covered several models between 1920 and 1926, but his most successful one had a forty-horsepower engine and two rotors, coaxially mounted. The most interesting part of his design was his biplane-type rotor blades. Instead of using individual blades, he attached them in pairs one above the other, like the biplane arrangement that used to be so common in fixed-wing aircraft. He had a propeller in the nose of the ship for forward motion. Many flights, several minutes long, were made, but once more lack of stability seems to have been the major bugbear.

In 1930, a Dutchman named von Baumhauer undertook a helicopter project that received much adverse comment. Yet

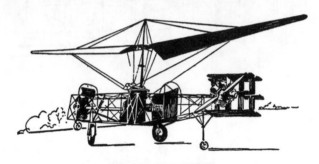

THE VON BAUMHAUER.

it was fundamentally of the same type as the successful Sikorsky models. Von Baumhauer used a single large main rotor driven by a 200-horsepower engine. To compensate for torque, he had an auxiliary propeller at the tail, mounted in the vertical plane like the ordinary aircraft rudder. This propeller exerted a sideways pull on the tail to keep the fuselage from whirling in a direction opposite to that of the main rotor. It was driven by a separate eighty-horsepower engine, although it is not clear why the calculations indicated that so much power was needed. In the present Sikorsky design, a much smaller percentage of total power is required.

It is unfortunate that von Baumhauer's machine was damaged before it could be well proved. This circumstance left the door open for critics to point out that such a design was a good example of how not to tackle the problem.[1] The Si-korsky success with the type vindicates von Baumhauer in his efforts.

About this same time an Italian named d'Ascanio came out with a ninety-five-horsepower ship that showed much prom-ise. He had two main rotors, coaxially mounted; and control was provided by three small auxiliary propellers. His craft

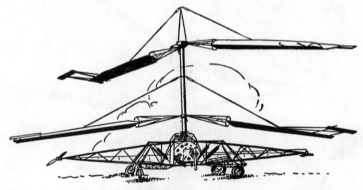

THE D'ASCANIO.

seemed to fly reasonably well, and he broke several earlier records, including that of duration with a flight of 8 minutes, 45 seconds.

Breguet was now returning to the helicopter field, and in 1935 he constructed a coaxial-rotored craft with 350 horse-power. He utilized many of the principles that had been de-veloped in Autogiro rotors and achieved notable results in control and stability. Many students of the subject believe that Breguet should be credited with the first truly successful helicopter. His machine suffered from being overweight, but it gave him sufficient confidence in the type to prepare a

[1] The chief criticism was based on the well-known engineering axiom that you cannot compensate a moment with a force. However, by the simple expedient of inclining the main rotor, a couple is created that effectively does the job.

scientific paper on a huge high-speed transoceanic helicopter flying boat. In view of Breguet's background of experience and proved ability, this paper created considerable interest, although a helicopter of this magnitude is still beyond the realm of present probabilities.

THE BREGUET.

In Germany, Dr. Heinrich Focke was also active with a design that, in 1937, stirred the world with its success. Focke used two contra-rotating rotors mounted on outriggers, one on each side of the fuselage. During the next two years the ship was widely demonstrated, including a series of flights within the Sports Palast at Berlin. It established a series of international records:

> Duration.  1 hour, 20 minutes, 49 seconds
> Distance (airline).  143.069 miles
> Distance (closed circuit).  50.085 miles
> Altitude.  11,243.416 feet
> Speed for 20 kilometers.  76.151 miles per hour

Focke developments since 1938 have not been announced. It is reported that German helicopters were used in the invasion of Holland. Word has also drifted back through the grapevine that the Focke type developed undesirable vibrations and could not hold together for many hours of flight. Confirmation or denial must undoubtedly await the ending

FOCKE FW-61 (EXPERIMENTAL STAGE).

of the war, but in the meantime, credit must be extended for an excellent step forward in helicopter development.

The foregoing helicopter history is a brief report of my introduction to the work that had gone before. Armed with this background, I was better prepared to understand the problems that confronted us in our own efforts. Frankly, I was mystified. It was difficult to see why Mr. Sikorsky had succeeded where so many had failed. I was disturbed by the thought that perhaps failure was even then lurking over our heads; that we might suddenly come face to face with some totally insurmountable obstacle, as others must have done before us.

But back of our efforts stood the unswerving faith of Mr. Sikorsky. I believe now that his success can be charged to his calm, forceful, sometimes dogged confidence coupled with sound engineering and intuitive judgment.

Nevertheless, I had had a warning regarding possibilities, and I set to work finding out all I could for the job in hand.

## Chapter V

## RECORDS FOR AMERICA

O UT IN THE SHOP IT WAS DIFFICULT TO FIND THE HELI-
copter. Several experimental projects were being
initiated by the Vought-Sikorsky Division, and all
were housed in the relatively small experimental hangar. To
reach the VS-300, it was necessary to pick one's way through
an entire machine shop and among a great quantity of test
rigs, mock-ups, and miscellaneous components of strange-
looking craft.

Here was a complete airplane fuselage, hanging a couple
of feet off the floor, with what appeared to be tons of weights
fastened all over it. Some day soon, when the engineers and
instruments were ready, someone would pull a release and
the whole business would come crashing down to prove the
designed strength of the structure.

Nearby was a mock-up of a new model. It was almost finished, and at first glance it seemed about ready to take off.
But a mock-up lives an earth-bound World's Fair sort of life.
It is built in the quickest way possible, using whatever materials are easiest to get. It is sleek and polished only for a
short time, while the engineers and pilots review the work in
full scale and correct many minor items that might not be
discovered from blueprints. It is cut and patched, re-worked
here, completely changed there, until the results are satisfactory to all. Thereafter it is relegated to a dusty corner and
the veneer begins to crack and peel away, while the living aircraft for which it was the full-scale model takes shape. Then

one day, its usefulness gone, it is carted away to make room
for some shiny newcomer.

Beyond the mock-up, other structural tests were in various
stages of progress. A wing panel was loaded to measure its
deflection. A box spar and a truss section were being worked
on. And a heavy canvas curtain marked off a holy of holies
in which was some ultrasecret project that could be viewed
by no one but those directly associated with it.

In the far corner, at last, was the VS-300. Three or four
mechanics were carefully going over her, making a few
changes before the next flight, and checking every last detail
of her structure.

Beside her stood the mock-up of the ship being built for
the Army. It was fairly complete, but there were many details still to be settled. The cabin, for instance; should it be
rounded or square? If rounded, it would weigh several
pounds more, and weight was already a serious consideration. Then the main pitch lever—where should it be located?
And what would be the best way to install the instrument
panel so it would cause the least interference with vision?

To answer these and a multitude of similar questions, Mr.
Sikorsky and the engineers were in a state of almost perpetual
conference. I hung around the outer fringe to listen, observe,
and study. This was to be my major assignment for two
months, because Mr. Sikorsky had one very important flight
to make in the VS-300. There had never been any official
American Endurance Record established for helicopters, and
Mr. Sikorsky proposed to set one. Even if he stayed in the
air for only half an hour, it would remain forever on the
books as a *first*. With this in view, it was obvious that I could
not expect to start flying for a while. No chances could be
taken until the record flight was over.

The date was finally set for April 15, and on the ninth,
Mr. Sikorsky made his last flights in preparation for the event.

Fuel consumption was carefully checked. Engine cooling was investigated with flights increasing in length up to as much as fourteen minutes. When it was over, the machine was returned to the shop for thorough inspection, weighing, and cleaning up.

We were keeping our fingers crossed for a pleasant day and a fresh wind on the fifteenth. Rain would be most unwelcome, because the VS-300's mechanism and pilot were exposed to the elements. The wind we wanted, because a helicopter requires much less power to move through the air than to hover at zero air speed. With a wind, it would be possible to stay over one spot on the ground, and still reap the benefits of using lower power—benefits realized in reduced fuel consumption and better engine cooling.[1]

If we had had the weatherman on our staff, the day could not have been more satisfactory. It dawned bright and clear, and by noon a fifteen-mile wind was blowing steadily out of the southwest. We were told it would stay with us all afternoon.

At three o'clock, Mr. Sikorsky stepped into the seat and started the engine, while William C. Zint, directing official for the National Aeronautics Association, outlined the standard requirements. The official witnesses—Walter Goddard, Treasurer of the Stratford Bank, and William St. John, Stratford druggist—stood in readiness for their roles.

Finally, at 3:08 P.M., Mr. Sikorsky opened the throttle and raised the craft from the ground. The stop watches and cameras clicked as he held the wheels three or four feet high and trimmed the controls for the long flight. From then on, it was only a matter of letting the minutes roll by until a land-

---

[1] Helicopters need the most power for hovering at zero air speed, for full forward flight, and for climbing. At intermediate speed ranges (presently about 15 to 70 m.p.h.), level flight can be maintained with about 60 to 75 per cent of the power required for hovering.

ing would be necessary because of the limited gas supply—
or until some other unforeseen development should cut things
short.

To relieve the monotony, Mr. Sikorsky would sometimes
climb straight upward for twenty or thirty feet and hang
there awhile. Then he would drop down again or move off
to one side or the other. Occasionally he would pose the ship
in the air for a picture. But, on the whole, it was simply
watch and wait.

When half an hour had passed, we all began to breathe
more freely. No matter how short the flight had been, it
would have established a record; but certainly it would look
better to have a respectable amount of time in the books.

Three quarters of an hour—and we began to watch the gas
level as indicated in the glass gauge at the end of the fuel
tank. How much longer would he be able to stay up?

When the one-hour mark was reached, we decided it was
time to let well enough alone, and we signaled him to land.
He nodded with a happy smile, but he wanted to add just a
little bit more flying for the sake of the record. Finally, after
1 hour, 5 minutes, 14½ seconds, his wheels again touched the
ground. Here was a substantial performance, the like of
which had never been even unofficially approached in the
Western Hemisphere. Congratulations were warmly exchanged among the pilot, the engineers, and the crew.

I didn't know until later that this was not the end of records. The following day Major Gregory and Captain Haugen
(they had been promoted) arrived, and they were offered
another fling at the controls. The ship was taken to the little
meadow back of the plant, and Mr. Sikorsky began with a
brief demonstration flight. After a few minutes his attention
suddenly focused on the little wind indicator that had been
stuck up in the ground. It was a six-foot pole with a small
metal ring mounted on top to hold a miniature wind-sock.

Carefully he flew the machine toward it. Then, with great precision and skill, he manipulated the nose boom of the helicopter through the ring and lifted the pole out of the ground. It was a masterly job, well timed and well executed—and right there was born one of the favorite demonstrations that we have used hundreds of times to show the controllability of our craft.

Gregory and Haugen both flew that day, and, although they had not been at the controls for many months, they quickly revived their technique and spent the better part of half an hour in the air, trying out the ship's flying qualities.

After they had finished, Mr. Sikorsky said, "Major Gregory, we have just received the new flotation bags for water operation. They are ordinary pneumatic bags, like the rubber boats that are being made these days. We haven't yet tested them, but if you would like, we could install them for tomorrow and see how they act."

It was a queer-looking contraption that was taken, next day, to the bank of the river. Two large green sausages formed the major part of the undercarriage. Beneath the tail was a smaller, supplementary sausage—and under the nose was a white rubber bladder from a basketball! Mr. Sikorsky himself, wearing an awkward quilted life jacket, was quite in keeping with the craft's padded appearance, except for the gray fedora hat perched on top of his head.

But looks were secondary to the job in hand. The ship was carried to the water's edge and set afloat as a preliminary test to be certain that the gear was adequate to support the weight and was properly balanced. Once this was determined, the engine was started, and Mr. Sikorsky stepped aboard.

After he had satisfied himself that everything was in order, we pushed him out into the river and he was on his own. He tried the controls and soon discovered that he could taxi on the water quite readily. He could move forward, come to a stop, or turn about in his tracks. He had all the maneuverability of a surface craft—plus!

When he had completed that investigation, he opened the throttle, pulled up a little on the pitch control and took off. He made three brief flights without incident, each time landing gently on the water. Finally he glanced in toward the meadow. After analyzing the situation, he decided to attempt a landing on the ground with no wheels to help him—only the rubber floats. As he flew in, we dashed up the river bank; and we scrambled over the top just in time to see the ship settling vertically and gently into the grass.

Thus, on April 17, 1941, Mr. Sikorsky and the VS-300 recorded what were, so far as we know, the world's first water flights of a helicopter, and also the first amphibian flight. The rubber pontoons had proved so successful that it was obvious we would have to plan on this becoming a popular and practical landing gear. Gregory and Haugen shared this view and asked that we give some thought to designing the ship we were building for the Army to accommodate a pontoon undercarriage.

Things were still humming, though. The American Endurance Record was only fifteen minutes short of the international record held by the Focke-Wulf in Germany, and Mr. Sikorsky decided that, with one alteration, the VS-300 could exceed that time by an appreciable margin. All that was needed was a little more gas—three or four gallons would be enough. So an oversized fuel tank was constructed, and arrangements were made to go after the World's Record on May 6.

Again the weather was good to us. It was a clear day with a ten-mile wind. Mr. Zint returned with Mr. J. P. V. Heinmuller as directing officials, and Messrs. Goddard and St. John once more served as witnesses. For these flights the press

had been invited, and a large number of reporters, cameramen, and newsreel operators were present.

About noon, Mr. Sikorsky took off for a trial flight, to be
sure no last-minute adjustments were required, and he utilized the opportunity to pose the ship for photographs and
movies.

Then, while the last cupful of gas was being squeezed into
the tank, he spoke briefly to the press. "The present flight,"
he said, "is made not as an attempt to demonstrate spectacu-
lar characteristics, but rather as a scientific laboratory test
intended to prove certain novel principles of flying. There
are tens of thousands of aircraft in the United States whose
flight and control are based on more or less rapid movement
through the air. There is probably no other aircraft in the
Western Hemisphere whose flight and control are thoroughly
and completely independent of its motion through the air.
You are about to witness the most unspectacular event you
have ever covered. All that I propose to do is to take off and
hang stationary over a spot for about an hour and a half.
There will be no tricks, no stunts—just plain hovering."

The engine was started again, and the timers waited for the
split second when the landing gear would leave the ground.
This came at 1:16:30 P.M.

For several minutes I wasn't sure whether or not it might
be a false start. The ship's wheels were wavering one to three
feet above the ground, and the engine was obviously putting
out its last ounce of power. There were 14.7 gallons of gas
on board. This doesn't sound like much in terms of large
airplanes, but it was 4.7 gallons more than she had carried
for the American record, and it meant twenty-eight pounds
of extra load. We knew that if the wind slacked off before
some of the fuel was used up, a landing would be almost
inevitable.

But Mr. Sikorsky didn't try to force more power; he just

held her where she was, and after five minutes or so the reduction in weight began to show up in the expanding air gap between the ground and the wheels. Now he had five feet clearance, and after a few minutes more the margin was ample and our worries were over.

Our only problem then was to keep ourselves amused while the time rolled slowly on. At first it was easy; the company had provided a couple of cafeteria wagons with sandwiches and coffee. Then for a time we watched an impromptu soccer game that the crew was playing with the basketball that had comprised the ship's nose gear during the water flights.

The pilot, though, was given little chance for relaxation. The cameramen quickly sensed the easiest way to do their job, and instead of dashing around to get just the correct angle, light, or background, they would leisurely set up a camera for the scenery they wanted and then signal Mr. Sikorsky to "move over just a trifle, please," or "turn the ship a little more to the left, sir," or "just a foot or two higher, if you will," until the composition suited them. It was a rare opportunity to make an aircraft in flight pose at their direction.

But photographers have a way of not recognizing hazards— or perhaps they simply disregard them. Several times they got practically under the ship to take a shot directly upwards. One man lay on his back and signaled for the craft to hover over him, which Mr. Sikorsky finally did, in spite of some misgivings for the individual's safety.

When at last the time of the American endurance record was exceeded, we grouped ourselves in a wide semicircle in front of the ship and counted the minutes that were left. Fifteen minutes more would equal the international record. How much longer could he stay up?

Labensky, with his habitual foresight, had a pair of binoculars and, with the ship only seventy-five feet away, we could

WORLDS RECORD
BROKEN
1 HOUR 20 MIN

MR. SIKORSKY BRINGS TO AMERICA THE INTERNATIONAL ENDURANCE RECORD FOR HELICOPTERS. (NOTE THE OVERSIZED GASOLINE TANK BEHIND HIS RIGHT SHOULDER.)

MR. SIKORSKY PILOTS THE VS-300 AS THE WORLD'S FIRST AMPHIBION HELI-
COPTER (SEE P. 47).

THE AUTHOR DEMONSTRATES PRECISION CONTROL BY "SPEARING THE RING" EXACTLY IN THE CENTER.

THE AUTHOR TESTS THE "PARTIAL AZIMUTHAL CONTROL." THE TOWER ABOVE THE TAIL SUPPORTS A CONTROL ROTOR THAT GOVERNS THE FORE-AND-AFT TILTING OF THE CRAFT. THE "AZIMUTH PLATE," JUST BELOW THE MAIN ROTOR HUB, PROVIDES CYCLICAL PITCH CHANGE OF THE MAIN ROTOR BLADES.

THE FUSELAGE IS PARTLY COVERED TO TEST THE EFFECT OF FIN-AREA.

read the gas gauge almost to an ounce. We studied the indicator and hastily calculated fuel consumption and balance available.

Finally, with the speed of a turtle, 1 hour and 20 minutes crept by, and the sign that had been painted to inform the pilot, "World's Record Broken," was made ready. As the timers signaled that the German record was exceeded, it was raised in front of Mr. Sikorsky.

He smiled happily and nodded his appreciation to the applauding group below.

From then on, the tension was relieved. Mr. Sikorsky stayed only three or four feet above the ground so that, in case the gasoline should run out unexpectedly, he could still make a satisfactory landing. But after another ten minutes, a hollow sort of pounding noise began to develop in the engine. We were concerned that something serious might be going wrong. With the record well in hand, it seemed the wiser course to cut it short, even though there were still over 2½ gallons of gas left in the tank.

So at 2:48:56.1 P.M., the wheels again touched the ground, bringing to America the new International Helicopter Endurance Record of 1 hour, 32 minutes, 26.1 seconds.

## Chapter VI

### I AM FLEDGED

NOW THAT THE RECORD FLIGHTS WERE OVER, I WAS EAGER to get started with my job as test pilot; and I hadn't long to wait. On May 12, the ship was out again, and I felt certain that this day would see me flying the helicopter for the first time.

At the outset, Mr. Sikorsky ran a series of tests to try to track down our omnipresent problem: the occasional *wobbling* and reduction of control in forward flight. But after lunch, Serge Gluhareff had a crack at it—he had not done much flying for several months—and I knew my chance was next.

When Gluhareff was through, Mr. Sikorsky took me to the ship.

"Try it out gently, Les," he advised. "Take plenty of time and remember above everything else, if you run into trouble, just throw the pitch lever down and land. You may land hard; you may even do some minor damage to the craft. But it will be better than having things go out of control higher in the air."

He showed me where to set the throttle and how much pitch to use for flight. Then he left me to work out my own salvation.

Uppermost in my mind was the picture of Gregory and Haugen rocking from side to side. I was sure that I would profit from having watched them and that lateral overcontrol would be one error I wouldn't make.

Slowly I opened the throttle, and the power built up. The

first thing was to feel out the fore-and-aft control by lifting the tail off the ground and balancing on the wheels. This freed the tail so it could turn, giving me an opportunity to investigate the rudder pedals too, but it eliminated for the time being the sideways control and the question of height above the ground. I spent several minutes just coordinating the first two movements, so that when the ship should finally take off, I could concentrate my full attention on the other two.

Finally I decided that things were satisfactorily in hand, and very slowly I began to increase the pitch, still keeping the ship balanced on the main wheels. In a few seconds it began to lift. Everything was going beautifully; I wasn't rocking, and I began to be quite proud of my showing. I held it steady for three or four minutes, and at last decided I could hazard a quick glance at the wheels to see how high I was.

My pride burst like a bubble when I discovered that the wheels were still on the ground! The landing-gear shock struts had extended, telescope fashion, when the ship had begun to lift, so that, although I myself was a few inches higher, I could lay no claim to actual flight.

With considerable chagrin, I pulled up further on the pitch control and felt the ship rise again. I was beginning to wonder if I would know when I was in the air without taking another look at the wheels, but the question answered itself. The craft began to drift sideways, and I moved the stick to counteract it. It responded much more briskly than I had anticipated, so I hastily jerked the stick the other way. And before I knew what was happening, I was rocking merrily from side to side, in true beginner's fashion.

I ignominiously availed myself of the solution that Mr. Sikorsky had mentioned, slapped down the pitch control, and landed—on one wheel, to be sure, but with no damage other

than a completely deflated ego. I set about to restore my
status, both to myself and to the amused onlookers. Slowly
I repeated the preliminaries and gently cleared the ground.
But the instant I was air-borne, that confounded rocking
started again.

After numerous trials, each one lasting perhaps a second
or two longer than the one before, I was able to make appreciable flights. They were always accompanied, however,
by an embarrassing amount of wobbling and bouncing, as
well as up-and-down uncertainty such as might be expected
of an old-fashioned elevator in the hands of an inexperienced
operator.

By the end of my workout, I had gained two distinct impressions. One was the delicate sensitivity of the controls. It
was something like riding a spirited horse with a very quick
response to the slightest pressure on the bit.

The other impression had to do with the *ground cushion.*
Even in fixed-wing airplanes, a cushion of *condensed air*
builds up between the wing and the ground. This is particularly noticeable in low-wing types when they are landing,
and the cushion causes them to float for some distance across
the field. In the helicopter, the cushion can be felt when the
rotor is at a height above the ground equivalent to not more
than about half its diameter. For instance, if the diameter is
thirty feet, the ground effect is apparent for about fifteen
feet. However, it is determined, not by the height of the
wheels, but by the height of the rotor. In the VS-300, the
ship itself was about ten feet tall, so the ground cushion was
present until the wheels were about five feet off the ground.

After I had begun to get the ship a little more under control so I could think about something besides stick and rudder,
pitch and throttle, I noticed that this cushion appeared to
burst when I reached an altitude of four or five feet. Two
things happened: first, the ship would start to settle slightly;

and, second, I would feel an up-gust of air around me. Further investigation proved that, if the controls were not changed at all, the ship would settle only a foot or two before the cushion would rebuild itself, with the result that we would gently oscillate up and down like a very slow-motion bouncing ball.

My first day with the helicopter was full of kaleidoscopic reactions which took a month or more to get sorted out. During this time, I logged about two and a half hours' flying, involving a great deal of just plain training, as well as a small number of minor flight investigations. Much of our work concerned the center of gravity of the ship and the height and length of the tail outriggers, all in an attempt to isolate the chronic wobbling in forward flight. Control reaction was also analyzed; and the oil dampeners on the main rotor blades were removed to check again whether we really needed them. Apparently we didn't—at least for the time being.

We investigated the effect of *fin-area*, to discover whether control would be helped or hindered by fuselage covering. I was struck dumb by the process. The entire tail of the craft was beautifully bedecked with clean airplane fabric, stretched drumtight by *doping*. After we had each made a few flights and recorded our impressions, someone coolly produced a jackknife and, at the direction of Mr. Sikorsky, began slashing off great sections of the cloth. Then, with the tattered edges flapping in the wind, flights were resumed to see whether it was better or worse with reduction in covered area. The craft was thus progressively denuded until the bare frame was once more fully exposed, and the fabric that had been so painstakingly applied lay torn and useless in the rubbish barrel.

One point that had a great deal of continuing attention was the so-called *throttle synchronization*. Every time the pilot would change the pitch of the main blades to go up or down, the load on the engine would change. More pitch required more power, and vice versa. It was too much to expect that a pilot whose hands and feet were already quite fully occupied with controls could simultaneously operate the throttle with each slight alteration in pitch. Therefore, a mechanical hookup was incorporated in the pitch-control system, in an attempt to make the throttle work automatically. The difficulty was to mix just the proper amount of the two ingredients for all conditions of flight, and we spent many hours on adjustments and modifications.

Toward the end of June, we embarked on a program to return by easy stages to the type of control system that had been used at the very outset—*azimuthal control*. This system had undoubtedly been the cause of Gluhareff's accident, but if its shortcomings could be eliminated, it would offer many tempting advantages. The primary ones were simplification of controls and of the power transmission system, as well as elimination of the horizontal tail outriggers which were both awkward and ugly. With such a change, we could hope to achieve full forward flight, which was apparently out of the question as long as we retained the horizontal-control rotors.

Admittedly, azimuthal control would be difficult to perfect. If anyone doubted this point, he was invited to review the early moving pictures that were taken in slow motion to minimize the severity of bouncing, rocking, and pitching. But for all that, it was well worth trying again.

Since azimuthal control is now used on all Sikorsky machines, and has apparently been universally adopted by the dozens of embryonic helicopter developments throughout the country, a word of explanation is in order. What we wanted to accomplish was to tilt the main rotor by its own action, rather than by bodily rolling or rocking the fuselage. This tilting of the rotor could be done by *feathering*, or changing the pitch of the blades as they turned. As a blade feathers to

### AZIMUTHAL CONTROL ACTION
(The tilting of the fuselage is exaggerated in these sketches)

**FORWARD** ⟹

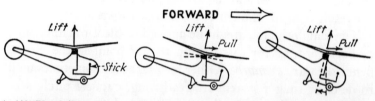

In HOVERING, the control stick is NEUTRAL, so the rotor gives only vertical lift

When the stick is moved FORWARD, the rotor tilts, giving some horizontal PULL

As the craft begins to move, the fuselage tilts too, so that the stick returns to neutral in the ship, though still inclined in relation to the ground

**BACKWARD** ⟹

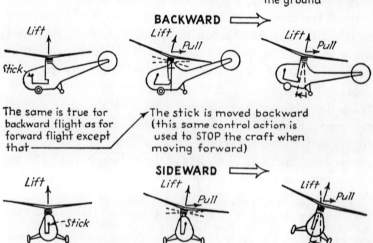

The same is true for backward flight as for forward flight except that ⟶

The stick is moved backward (this same control action is used to STOP the craft when moving forward)

**SIDEWARD** ⟹

If you will study this last series for a moment you will see that the only change from the FORWARD and BACKWARD sketches is that the fuselage is pointing toward you. The stick and the rotor, however, have done exactly the same thing in each of three cases high pitch, it begins to ride higher; with low pitch, it flattens out and rides lower. If the highest point in the cycle is above the tail of the craft, and the lowest point is over the nose, the net result is to tilt the entire rotor disk forward.

The same principle might be applied to tilt it to either side, or backward, or for that matter, to any point in the circle: hence the term *azimuth*. (Other terms that are sometimes used to describe such a system are feathering, cyclical pitch, sectional, progressive pitch, direct pitch, or reflex control.) [1]

We knew what was wanted, but we also knew what we already had. The problem was to make the transition from one to the other with the greatest possible safety.

A so-called *azimuth plate* was installed around the shaft beneath the main rotor, and some rods from the blades were attached to it so that, when the plate was tilted, it would bring about the required feathering. This much was comparatively simple. But to make it work properly required seemingly endless readjustments, revisions, and test investigations. Throughout July we struggled with the experimental rig, tried it in the hangar and on the field, made brief, cautious flights, and studied the results. Some of them were favorable—many were downright bad. But analysis always seemed to indicate that our troubles stemmed from the fact that we were

[1] For the benefit of the mechanically inquisitive, the means by which this function is accomplished may be briefly described. On the main rotor shaft, just below the hub, there are two plates attached to each other in sandwich fashion. The filling for the sandwich is a bearing that permits the top plate to rotate while the bottom one stays stationary. From each of the three corners of the top plate, a short push-pull link goes up to an arm on one of the blades. If the sandwich remains perpendicular to the shaft, therefore, the blades will turn without changing pitch. If, however, the plate is tilted, the push-pull links will follow this inclined plane, in a kind of *cam* or *swash-plate* action. As each link goes to the lower portion of the tilted plate, it will pull downward on the arm attached to its respective blade and will thus reduce its pitch. As the link rides upward along the incline, it will push the arm up and cause the blade pitch to increase.

still reluctant to discard entirely the horizontal outriggers at the tail, and the two systems just didn't blend.

It was decided at last to take a long step and remove the offending outriggers. However, we were not yet prepared to go the whole way. We would retain one horizontal propeller at the tail for fore-and-aft control, mounting it directly above the fuselage. Thus we would restrict our initial experiments to the investigation of feathering only as it applied to lateral control, or "rolling."

The re-work was finished early in August, and Mr. Sikorsky made two short hops, discovering a few minor adjustments that were required. The following day, as we walked out to the airport, he said to me, "Would you like to try her first, today?" This was my first opportunity to do the initial testing of a new arrangement, and the answer was written on my face. He smiled in fatherly fashion as he carefully reviewed what I should watch for.

One thing worried me, though: the ship had no wheel brakes. We had always used the metal tail skid to give us a braking effect, but in the redesign we had installed a tail *wheel*, and I was concerned about the possibilities—particularly since there was a fairly strong wind that might roll the machine backward over the hard pavement.

For starting, I had the crew put a small sandbag behind each main wheel. "That's fine," said Plenefisch, "but what will you do when you land?"

"I'll try to set the wheels down just in front of the bags," I replied, "and settle back onto them. If I can't do it, I'll shake my head and one of your fellows can stand by each wheel so that when I touch down he can drop a sandbag behind it."

The take-off was no trouble, and I enjoyed immeasurably the opportunity to inquire into the functioning of this new control, entirely on my own. I hovered for a short time, feeling out the sensitivity, the neutral positions, the period of

time required for a given motion to take effect. Then I crept
slowly forward, stopped, and drifted backward. Slow sideways flight was next—and as everything appeared in order
and I got the feel of the ship, I undertook more advanced
maneuvers, going out across the airport at ten to fifteen miles
an hour and completing a slow figure-eight, ending up at
the sandbags.

Then I thought it was time to try my skill at landing. I
hovered, looking back at the wheels and trying to hold them
as close as I could to the foot-square bags on the ground.
Several times I started to descend, only to find that I was
drifting slightly one way or the other. But at last I managed
to drop the wheels gently a few inches from the bags, and
they nestled back onto them for a victorious climax.

After a second, longer flight, another sandbag landing was
attempted. I am afraid I was flushed and confident with the
first success. I thought I was taking ample time, but I was
watching only the left wheel, and the right one landed *on*
the sandbag. I felt the difference in height as the ship tilted
over, and in my confusion I moved too many controls at
once—with the result that the tail wheel struck the ground
a sidewise blow and buckled up.

The tail rotor beat the macadam and flew into a hundred
pieces. It was completely unbalanced then, and the entire
ship began to shudder violently. I couldn't imagine what had
gone wrong, but I reached for the ignition switch and shut
off the engine.

This was my first accident with a helicopter. As I stood
viewing the damage, minor though it was, I felt the weight
of it deeply, particularly since I confess that the sandbag
landing contained some element of show-off. Mr. Sikorsky
must have sensed my feelings. "Never mind, Les," he said,
"if that's the worst you will ever do, it will be good."

Within a couple of days we were out at the airport again,

and almost immediately the ship was found to be very fly-able. Control was excellent under all conditions. Carefully we pushed into unexplored realms, going a little faster with each flight, turning a little more sharply, stopping or maneuvering with a little more snap. We were constantly on the alert for evidence of control difficulties, but to our growing wonderment they failed to appear.

During this day, August 14, 1941, we saw the VS-300 emerge from its cocoonlike state, spread its flimsy, unproven wings, and discover itself as a true flying craft. Slowly through our minds there may have filtered a dim hint as to what this meant. For myself, I know that as the ship unfalter-ingly responded to my touch, swept low over the airport, swung in graceful curves, or hung motionless above a spot on the ground, I gained a new and vastly reassuring concep-tion of the whole program.

For centuries, man had dreamed of such a vehicle. For several decades, capable engineers had been groping for the solution. Mr. Sikorsky himself had spent just one month less than two years intensively struggling with the problem. Now, so suddenly that we failed to grasp its full meaning, we found ourselves in possession of the answer. An obviously successful helicopter had been achieved!

There was one thing about our work, however, that was often disheartening. The VS-300 was not expected, neces-sarily, to become a flying aircraft. Its fundamental destiny was as an instrument for experimentation. Therefore, when results were good, it was not possible to leave well enough alone; we would immediately lay plans for changes. Always, of course, their purpose was to make the craft even better. Frequently that was achieved. But frequently, too, the op-posite would occur, and we would scratch our heads for causes, experiment with changing the changes, and finally, perhaps, after weeks of effort, charge off the net results to profit and loss—and experience.

Thus, in keeping with her destiny, the VS-300 ended her first day of real life by being returned to the shop for a month of much-needed grooming and a couple of major rearrangements. When she again took to the air, a flock of "bugs" had been hatched that required several days to exterminate. Soon, however, the net results of the month's work could be evaluated, and there was no doubt that this time the balance sheet showed a profit.

If the craft was flyable in August, it was beautiful now. "Beautiful," of course, refers to flying qualities, not to looks. In appearance it was still the same awkward, bare-limbed creature; still scoffed at by many, although beginning to assume new stature in the eyes of some earlier skeptics as they saw performances of an amazing sort.

Demonstrations became the order of the day for distinguished visitors to the plant. Extensive flights were made to record in moving pictures the inimitable maneuvers and the smooth flying qualities of this newly awakened machine.

During one of these demonstrations, I experienced my second mishap. I had been flying at speeds estimated as high as seventy miles an hour, making a series of figure-eights about twenty-five feet above the ground. As I attempted to recover from one of the steep turns, I lost most of my speed, and this reduced the lift of the rotor. As the craft settled, I reached for the throttle, but it was too late to do much good. I landed straight down with a rather severe jolt.

Honored guests were only a couple of hundred feet away, so I glanced around quickly at the tail of the fuselage to be sure it was still intact, then took off again and flew slowly over in front of them, where I set down once more and shut off the engine. I discovered, then, that they all thought the hard landing was intentional on my part—that I was demonstrating how quickly the ship could come to a stop and land—and I did not disillusion them.

Shortly, I asked Mr. Sikorsky if he wanted any more flights that day. "No, I don't think so," he replied. Then, as he drew me quietly to one side, "There is a bent tube in the fuselage."

I looked from where I was standing and could detect nothing. I carefully surveyed each tube separately, but still couldn't see it. Later, after the guests had departed, a close inspection revealed that one tube was bowed very slightly out of line. Yet Mr. Sikorsky must have spotted it from more than twenty-five feet away as soon as the ship landed!

In October, we put the craft back on rubber pontoons. We had had new ones made that were longer than the ones Mr. Sikorsky had first used in the spring. The ship's controls were different, too, since we had shed the tail outriggers.

The first day was full of interesting experiences for Gluhareff and me. It was one of those dead calm days when the Housatonic River was like a shimmering mirror. We found it very difficult to tell how high or how fast we were flying.

The glassy water, though, gave us an opportunity to watch the action of the down-wash of air from the rotor. Over land it had never been clearly discernible, but as we flew above the river we were shadowed by a widening trail of dark-blue ripples. When we slowed down, the ripples would creep closer to us, and as we came to a full stop they would get all mixed up for a few seconds and then would re-form into a perfect ring around the craft. The center of the ring was always fairly calm, since there was no appreciable down-wash from the middle portion of the rotor.

It was interesting, too, to land on the water. Even a hard landing could barely be felt. Once down, if we didn't watch the shore line or some stationary object, we had difficulty keeping the craft on a spot. The slightest tilt of the stick

would result in motion, but with no accompanying change
of engine sound or wind. This quality has baffled many experienced seaplane pilots who miss the slap of the waves on
the pontoons, the pressure of the rudder, and the varying
roar of the engine in response to throttle.

More recent experience has shown that the ripples around
the pontoons are an effective indication of the craft's drift.
But without some such guide, the pilot can feel peculiarly
insecure.

The flexibility of the machine as a surface vessel was nothing short of miraculous. The precision control that we had
found so apparent in flight was even more obvious on water.
In Mr. Sikorsky's first amphibious trials, he had demonstrated
forward and backward taxying and turning on a spot; but he
had not then been able to move sideways. Now, with the
new lateral azimuthal control, we could tilt the rotor without
having to tilt the entire craft, with the result that sideways
taxying was just as simple as the rest. When we wanted to
pull in to the dock, we could hold the pontoon within an
inch of the desired spot, regardless of wind or cross-current.
We could approach a channel buoy head on, sideways, or
tail first, as we wished, even with a six-mile tide running.

With all the good experiences of our first big day on pontoons, we could expect some adverse results too. On the last
flight, Gluhareff decided to set the ship down on land in
order to simplify the job of getting her back to the hangar.
He came in slowly over the ramp and, as the pontoons gently
touched in an excellent soft landing, the most extraordinary
things began to happen.

The ship started bouncing from one pontoon to the other
in increasing violence, with the pilot waving around in the
seat like a palm tree in a hurricane. He pushed down on the
main pitch control, as we had all been taught to do in case of
trouble, but his coat sleeve caught on the throttle handle and

opened the gas wide. The over-speeding engine made the rocking ten times worse, so he did the only thing left—he pulled up on the pitch again and shot up into the air. Once off the ground the shaking began to calm down, but Gluhareff, quite understandably confused by the unexpected performance, availed himself of a pilot's last resort and shut off the ignition switch. He dropped down hard from a height of about ten feet, and the tail section of the fuselage buckled from the impact so that the tail rotor struck the ground and tore itself to pieces.

Aside from a severe limbering up, the pilot appeared to be none the worse for the experience. This was our first lesson in *ground resonance*—a phenomenon familiar to rotary-wing aircraft—and on the basis of what we now know could have happened, we got it at a bargain.

Ground resonance may occur in a helicopter or Autogiro with the conventional blade arrangement, when the landing gear bounces the ship from side to side at exactly the right speed to be in harmony with the speed of the main rotor. On the first bounce, the rotor may be thrown somewhat out of balance, and each succeeding bounce makes it worse, until the tremendous energy stored in the rotor may at last literally tear the ship to pieces.

At the time of this experience, we knew that the problem could exist, but, never having found any trace of it in the VS-300, we had unwittingly removed the remedy for it some months before, when we took off the oil dampeners on the blades. Adequate dampeners counteract the unbalance that is created by the ground resonance, and without them we were exposed to trouble.

Repairs were finished within a week, but ill luck still dogged our footsteps. As we were warming up for the new flights, one of the tail rotor blades struck the fuselage and knocked off about three inches of the blade tip. We thought flights would have to be canceled again, until it was discovered that the wood hadn't split too far inboard. A saw was produced, some careful measurements taken, and the tip of the other blade was summarily cut off to match the damaged one! Flights proceeded as planned, with a slight reduction in rudder control, but with another bit of experience under our belts.

The following weeks were spent investigating thoroughly the qualities of the new control and giving an ever-increasing number of demonstrations to visitors from the aeronautical industry who refused to believe the stories about the VS-300, or even the films of her, and who had to come and see for themselves that the events we depicted were really happening. To foster the impression that this machine was now becoming an actual aircraft, we even built up a lightweight cowling for the nose. This helped to calm the fears of the skeptics who assumed that, since the pilot in this experimental craft sat in a completely exposed position, all future helicopters must be built the same way.

During one demonstration, I inadvertently made some sort of altitude record, when I reached an estimated 100 feet during a steep turn at sixty miles an hour. Altitude was not this craft's strong point. It had been cut to pieces so many times, re-worked, re-welded, and patched up that we had never attempted to fly her high. We knew that she could probably climb to a few thousand feet, but there was nothing to be gained from such a flight, and there would be so much lost if anything should go wrong! So we patiently left altitude to a newer craft, built for the job, and utilized the VS-300 in the work for which she was admirably suited: investigation of control, stability, maneuverability, and equally important, pilot training.

It was for these four reasons that the ship was doomed to undergo another vital change. We had been flying for several

DRESSED UP WITH NOSE COVERING.

MR. SIKORSKY TAKES A CLOSE-UP.

A TURN CLOSE TO THE TREES.

AZIMUTHAL CONTROL AT WORK (SEE P. 57). FLYING FORWARD, THE ENTIRE CRAFT INCLINES SOMEWHAT FORWARD, WHILE IN COMING TO A STOP OR FLYING REARWARD, THE OPPOSITE IS TRUE.

FULL AZIMUTHAL CONTROL, JANUARY, 1942. THE TAIL TOWER AND THE HORIZONTAL CONTROL ROTOR HAVE DISAPPEARED. (THE CIRCULAR DISK AT THE TAIL WAS A TEMPORARY TEST INSTALLATION.)

TIRE TROUBLE IS NO TROUBLE AT ALL!

months with the horizontal tail propeller to give us fore-and-aft control, and our flights had been eminently successful. But back in the hangar the new machine for the Army was taking shape with just the rudder propeller at the tail. Not only lateral control, but fore-and-aft control as well was to be provided by feathering the blades; in other words, *full* cyclical-pitch control.

Since this was an innovation that had not yet been tried, it behooved us to get some experience with it on the VS-300. The new ship would be larger and more powerful, and it would be full of completely unknown characteristics. We decided that much grief might be avoided if we simplified the picture by having at least a trained pilot with a tested type of control.

In spite of the obvious wisdom of the decision, it was with great regret that we put the ship in the hangar late in November and issued instructions to tear out the combination that had achieved such outstanding results.

On December 8, 1941, the day the United States declared herself at war with Japan, we rolled out the VS-300 with a control mechanism similar to the one on the new ship. It had been a fairly simple change-over to rig up the tilting plate below the rotor hub so that, instead of rocking only from side to side, it could be inclined in any direction whatsoever.

I climbed into the seat and, with the engine warmed up, began carefully to experiment with the new arrangement and to feel for potential trouble spots. I opened the throttle bit by bit, and at each new speed I moved the stick to test its effect on the craft. Once or twice, a slight rocking on the wheels became apparent, reminiscent of ground resonance; and before proceeding further, I made sure that it could be stopped by closing throttle and reducing pitch—always "keeping a door open behind me." It brought to mind the time I explored an uncharted cave: I didn't know what lay ahead, and I wanted to be reasonably sure of a way back.

Gradually, however, it became apparent that the ship, while far from perfect, was not going to exhibit any completely uncontrollable tendencies. So I increased pitch and throttle a little more and cleared the ground. All went well for perhaps three or four seconds until I moved the stick slightly to overcome some sideways drift. Instantly it began to rock with increasing violence, and I dropped it quickly back onto the ground.

I had been caught way off guard and could offer little information to supplement the observations of Mr. Sikorsky and the others who had witnessed the episode from nearby. We decided to take time out to think it over and in the interim to check the craft carefully for any undesirable play in the controls or in the main hub.

During the next week, several attempts were made to get back in the air. Theories were as plentiful as balloons at a New Year's Eve party—and usually met the same end. Those that were not exploded by preliminary scrutiny were quickly given an actual test on the VS-300. If any improvements were noted, they were not sufficiently pronounced to be convincing. Each time the ship would take off, we would hope for some sign of progress. Each time, after five or ten or fifteen unhappy seconds in the air, a landing would be mandatory.

As I became more used to the tossing around, I was able to extend the flights somewhat to see what would happen next. I attempted some slow forward flying and was surprised to find that, as long as I kept moving at a dogtrot speed, the trouble didn't seem to increase. But when I stopped, I had to land in a hurry before it got totally out of hand. One thing was consistently true: a peculiar slight vibration would invariably be felt four or five seconds before the real trouble began, thus giving me time to get prepared.

Investigations were the order of the day. Vibration specialists completely analyzed the natural frequencies of all parts of the craft: the rotor shaft, fuselage, and landing gear particularly. Finally, Mr. Sikorsky decided that it was the old story of having no blade dampeners.

The old oleo struts were recalled into active service, but this time they were attached in such a way as to damp the blades' oscillations in the horizontal plane. Like a miracle from the Dark Ages, this simple expedient turned the trick. To quote from the VS-300's logbook for December 31, "Flights were made forward, backward and sideways, and no wobble or resonance was discovered at any time." Thus, on the last day of 1941, another totally new control arrangement was successfully demonstrated on the VS-300.

The recapitulation for the year, written in the ship's log, tells the story:

During the year 1941 three totally different types of control were investigated, with a total time in the air of 28 hours, 35 minutes, 55 seconds.

The horizontal outriggers (for longitudinal and lateral control) were on the craft at the beginning of the year, and continued to be the arrangement until June 17. With this control, excellent hovering flights were made, and forward flights at low speed. At higher speeds, however, some control difficulties were encountered. With this control the following records were made (Mr. I. I. Sikorsky as pilot):

April 15, 1941—American Helicopter Endurance Record—1 hour, 5 minutes, 14.5 seconds
April 17, 1941—First recorded Amphibian or Seaplane Helicopter Flights
May 6, 1941—International Helicopter Endurance Record—1 hour, 32 minutes, 26.1 seconds

On June 27, experimentation began with azimuthal control, resulting in installing lateral azimuth but retaining one horizontal auxiliary propeller on a tower above the tail. With this ship, definite improvements were recorded in stability—and in forward flight all previous difficulties disappeared. Flights up to 60 m.p.h. and faster were recorded, and many hours were spent on pontoons. The only remaining troubles were the rather awkward tail structure and the troubles pertinent to ground resonance.

On December 8, flights began with a full azimuthal control, the tail tower being removed. While ground and air resonance became troublesome at the start (being subsequently controlled by blade dampeners), control was adequate and excellent. C.G.[1] location was found to be not nearly so critical as anticipated. On December 31, excellent flights were made that indicated promising results for 1942.

[1] The center of gravity—the balancing point of the craft.

## Chapter VII

## NEW MODEL—NEW HORIZON

THE "PROMISING RESULTS" THAT HAD BEEN INDICATED for 1942 began to materialize immediately. During January, the new control in the VS-300 was being whipped into shape, with frequent flight schedules to evaluate a continuous barrage of readjustments. It was the most fascinating bit of exploring I had ever done. Each day began with a hope of pushing a little farther into the shadow of the unknown—and we were seldom disappointed. Nearly every flight proved or disproved something, but, like the multi-headed Hydra, each time we lopped off one question mark, two more appeared in its place.

At the outset, we didn't bother with any fabric covering. However, our new ship for the Army—already with its engine and rotor running for preliminary ground investigation —was fully enclosed, and it was imperative that we discover as soon as possible what peculiarities we might expect from extra drag, *keel area*, and allied items. The nose covering, of course, would increase the air drag on the fuselage, and there was some concern that at higher speeds it might "trip us up," making the ship nose over beyond the power of the controls to correct it. If that should happen, a crash would be inevitable, so it is understandable that I approached the problem with deep caution and profound respect.

We soon had the VS-300 "dressed up" in shiny new fabric, and the first part of the schedule was the investigation of forward and backward flight. I would back far down the field, then start forward, slowly at first, but faster with each

71

trip. When a speed of twenty-five miles an hour was reached in these straight runs, I began making gentle S turns. No undesirable conditions became apparent with application of control, so the turns were made increasingly abrupt, until finally we were satisfied with this first phase of the tests.

It was then considered satisfactory to proceed with more advanced flying, and I started out over the meadow for a series of figure-eights at steadily higher speeds, until forty to fifty miles an hour was attained. Then the turns were tightened up, bit by bit, until they were quite steep.

During this phase, the only thing that bothered me at all was a pronounced tendency for the ship to lose altitude when turning to the right, and gain it when turning to the left. I found it necessary to use the main pitch control to compensate for this quirk. Subsequent analysis revealed that it was quite natural and that it had nothing whatsoever to do with the covering of the fuselage. It was simply that a right turn required an increase in the pitch of the tail rotor blades; the higher pitched blades required more power to turn them; the engine at a given throttle setting was producing a fixed amount of power; therefore, the extra power needed by the tail rotor was actually being stolen from the main rotor, and the ship consequently settled.

The converse, of course, was true for a left turn: surplus power released by less tail-rotor pitch was fed into the main rotor, causing the craft to climb.

For these tests, I had to record the position of the control stick. If at any time it should begin to move rearward, this would be the red flag, indicating that the ship was being forced to nose over. It would then be time to declare an armistice and analyze the situation.

Suffice it to say that, during a fairly tense half-hour of testing, no such results were encountered. However, I did have the opportunity to discover one more interesting quality of the helicopter. I was doing figure-eights, cross-wind at fifty to sixty miles an hour and not more than thirty feet off the ground. During each straight leg of the eight, I would lean down into the cockpit and strike a pencil mark on a scale attached to the control stick, so that at the conclusion of the tests I would have a complete record of the findings. All went well until one run when it took me a little longer than usual to make the mark. When I glanced up, I found a row of tall elm trees looming closer than I had anticipated. I put the ship in a steep turn and probably would have cleared the trees, but without much margin. So, for safety's sake, I pulled up on the main pitch control. Since the ship was banked over quite severely, this had the astonishing result of hauling us bodily away from the trees without tightening up the turn whatsoever. The onlookers said later that it seemed as if a powerful wind had suddenly burst out of the elms and puffed me away.

Interesting as were these tests with the VS-300, they were all pointing up to the really crucial event of our helicopter career: the flights of the new ship. It was designated the XR-4: X meaning experimental, R meaning rotary wing, 4 indicating the fourth Army contract for this classification of aircraft.

Many things were different in this machine. For one thing it was twice the size and had twice the power of its predecessor. It weighed about a ton, empty, had a 175-horsepower Warner engine and a rotor diameter eight feet greater than the VS-300. These three factors alone placed it in a completely novel category. We had succeeded in making one small helicopter flyable. Would we be able to achieve equally satisfactory results in this larger endeavor?

Besides power and size, other changes had been introduced. Chief among them was a new type of pitch-control lever between the cabin seats, with the throttle grip at the end of it.

To open and close throttle, you twisted this grip in much
the same way as in a motorcycle. The difficulty was to remember which way was open, and which closed (even mo-
torcycles haven't standardized it). So, for several weeks, I
had made it a point to sit in the cabin and operate it frequently, and to review it mentally while at my desk—or even
in the armchair at home—until it was so nearly second nature
that I couldn't make a mistake. This was an urgent necessity
because, once in the air, my mind would be far too occupied
with other more pressing matters than a simple mechanical
detail like that. On the other hand, that detail, if improperly
handled, could spell trouble: if things went wrong, for instance, and instead of closing the throttle to land I should
accidentally open it—and fly higher!

As though I hadn't enough to keep me busy, I foolishly
added one more needless complication to the assignment. In
the VS-300, I had always flown with the main pitch lever in
my left hand. However, the XR-4 was designed to be flown
from the left side, which meant that the pitch lever between
the seats was at my right. As I look back on it, I wonder why
I didn't follow Mr. Sikorsky's guarded hint and sit on the
side where all controls would be in their accustomed places.
But I didn't; and, while nothing serious came of it, it was
many hours before I mastered an inordinate desire to use the
wrong control at the right time!

Add to the above the fact that our two weeks' experience
with complete azimuthal control on the VS-300 was inade-
quate, to say the least, and it may help to explain my mental
condition as I sat in the XR-4 at noon on January 14, 1942,
and wondered if this would be the day I would take this
craft into the air for its first flight—this craft in which so
much time, money, and genius had been invested, and which
might lay the groundwork for so great a future.

For what seemed an endless time, we ran the rotor at various speeds with four men hanging onto the landing gear to prevent the ship from taking off. We checked for engine adjustment and general operation of the controls. We paid special attention to the action of the main rotor, to be sure that when we moved the stick ahead the rotor would tilt straight forward, not diagonally to one side or the other. We made certain that the rudder pedals would provide enough power. Most of all we tried the main pitch and throttle mechanism, up and down, up and down. Thank heaven for my armchair practice of recent weeks!

Finally Bob Labensky and Ralph Alex, Project Engineer and assistant, respectively, stated that, so far as they could see, the ship was ready to try a flight when it was all right with me. The signal was given to remove the chocks from under the wheels; I released the brakes and prepared for the job ahead.

I began slowly to open the throttle and pull up on the main pitch lever. The throttle synchronization, I had found, was not too good—constant readjustment of throttle was required for every change of pitch. When the ship began to feel light, I moved the control stick carefully forward, to raise the tail and balance on the wheels. The ship was rocking sideways rather severely, because we had not tried to get the main rotor blades too accurately in track (one blade would ride higher than the others). This roughness was transmitted to the control stick which was describing a circle timed with the main rotor. But bit by bit it was possible to pull the pitch level higher, and with each pull I could feel the ship come closer to flight.

At last the wheels began to dance gently on the ground, and one more pull of the pitch lever broke us loose. Instantly we began drifting sideways, and I moved the stick to correct it. But this ship was heavier than the VS-300—its reaction time was totally different. At first I undercontrolled, then went to the other extreme and moved the stick much too far. The controls were stiff, especially the rudder pedals. The main pitch lever was extremely heavy, and it required a constant strong pull to keep it from going down. The whole situation felt very much as if I were supporting the entire weight of the craft in one hand while trying to balance it very delicately with the other by means of a control stick that was performing fanciful gyrations in front of me.

While I was thus physically engaged in maintaining questionable mastery of a dubious situation, I was also making a hasty analysis as to just how dubious it was. With each swinging, or lurching, or turning, I would try to decide whether to control it, or whether to let it run its course, or whether to just plain land, pronto!

What a jerky flight this first one turned out to be! I knew it at the time, but when I saw the moving picture records, I wondered if the observers were, perhaps, even more concerned than I was about the outcome. At any rate, I had no opportunity to study their expressions and am therefore grateful to the cameraman who trained the finder on Mr. Sikorsky and recorded for a few seconds his joyful grin, his excited wave of the hand.

After what seemed an hour, but was actually only three minutes, I eased off my pull on the main pitch lever and the craft settled down for a landing. The engine purred contentedly while we exchanged congratulations for a job of excellent teamwork now coming to fruition.

Then we made readjustments to bring the blades in better track, to centralize the control stick which had been offset to one side and forward, and to improve synchronization and rudder stiffness. Gear cases and bearings were inspected for signs of overheating or improper functioning. All controls, all parts of the rotor hub were checked. When the work was finished, I took off for a second hovering flight of five and a half minutes, after which we adjourned for lunch and for a careful consideration of all findings.

At four o'clock, we were out again with several refinements, including one that was most helpful to the pilot: a strong spring on the main pitch lever to help pull it up. This relieved the constant load on my right arm and gave more freedom for maneuvering.

Four more flights were made, during which I pushed into a careful investigation of slow forward motion and stayed up once for more than seven minutes!

On this first day, we logged 25 minutes, 6 seconds with the wheels off the ground. This is perhaps something of a record for an experimental aircraft of such novel character— we should have had cause to be proud with as little as two or three minutes aloft.

Many problems were already making themselves apparent. The solutions to some were reasonably clear—but some were puzzling in the extreme. While Mr. Sikorsky sat down with Labensky, the Gluhareffs, Alex, and the rest to chart the next moves, Prof Sikorsky avidly bit into the figures I was able to furnish on blade angles, engine and rotor speed, manifold pressure, etc., and proceeded to masticate them with his prodigious slide-rule.

The record of this first day carries two references to difficulties that were destined to hound the XR-4 almost every minute of its unusually successful career. They were "lack of power troublesome," and "main transmission case quite warm." If I should be asked what was really not right in the XR-4, I think I should say no more and no less than that. As would be expected, there were many other imperfections, but they were of such a nature that the pilots would correct for them, or simply excuse them in so experimental a machine. Power and transmission troubles, on the other hand, were omnipresent sources of concern that were never wholly banished from the pilots' thoughts, and sometimes brought us unpleasantly close to an accident.

During the next two weeks, thirty-two flights were made, including a demonstration to Gregory who hurried East after hearing of our progress. We learned many things—tried a multitude of ideas and adjustments with emphasis on the throttle, main pitch lever, control stick, rudder, keel area, and rotor blade trim. By the end of January, the ship had accumulated 2 hours, 21 minutes in the air—phenomenal for an experimental helicopter—and I had taken Michael Gluhareff aloft as my first helicopter passenger.

Early in February, I had my first really close call with the XR-4. Our investigations had led us to believe that the excellent qualities of azimuthal control might be still further improved, especially for higher speeds, if we installed airplane-type control surfaces at the tail. We had made a few flights with a similar arrangement on the VS-300, but had reached no final conclusions as yet. So we decided to try it on the XR-4.

Unfortunately, the day was pretty gusty, and the turbulence was particularly severe by the river bank where I had to pull to a stop after each test run. During one stop, when the tail of the fuselage was quite low, a strong gust struck the airplane-type control surface and twisted the machine around quite violently.

My first thought was that, if the tail sideswiped the ground, it would certainly mean an accident. So I pulled up sharply on the main pitch lever, to get as much clearance as possible. For several seconds the tail lashed back and forth like an angry alligator, and the observers reported that once or twice the tail skid cleared the ground by only an inch or two. Mr. Sikorsky's face, they said, was a rosy purple. However, in due time, I found the situation returning to normal, and I hovered for a half-minute or so in order to fix clearly in mind the impressions and factual conditions surrounding the episode. Then I repeated the flight as accurately as I could, using the same air speed and control motion and stopping at the same point. After two or three more attempts, I was somewhat disappointed, but in some ways relieved, that I could not make it happen again.

By the end of these flights we had accumulated a great number of changes to be introduced. Some required a major operation, some were quite minor; but the entire program took the craft off flying status for nearly two months, with one exception. This was on March 7, when I flew for a half-hour to check the results of certain re-work that was intended to provide more control fore and aft and laterally. The findings were excellent, and the balance of the month was spent crossing off the other items of re-work on the agenda.

## Chapter VIII

## PERFORMANCE DEMONSTRATED

EVEN BEFORE WE WERE READY TO RESUME FLYING, WE began to feel the pressure of military requirements, which was to build up in an ever more impelling crescendo for the next two years. Gregory telephoned from Wright Field one day toward the end of March and said, "We have to get the XR-4 delivered as soon as we can. We want to have a demonstration of it before an Army board at Stratford first, and then fly it out here."

We called a hurried conference. "What date should we set for the demonstration?" we asked.

"The sooner, the better," he answered. "Can you make it early next month? How about the tenth?"

"Well," we replied, "it would be pressing things quite a bit. What do you want us to demonstrate?"

"Everything," he said. "We want to show the helicopter as a flying aircraft. We want to show its precision control; we want to prove that it can carry two people, or more, if possible; we want to demonstrate speed, forty, sixty, eighty miles an hour; and we want to show some altitude. We at least ought to get the ship over the tree-tops. I'd like to see it up to 500 or 1,000 feet anyway. But of course 5,000 feet would be excellent!"

We gasped. "But we haven't even found out yet how she handles in autorotation, when the engine quits. We have a lot of investigation still for forward speed. It seems too early to set a date."

"Nonsense!" was his answer. "Suppose we make it April

80

20. That will give you practically a full month to learn all you need to."

We acquiesced—with our fingers crossed and a few extra rabbits' feet tucked in our pockets! The ship had a total of only three and one-half flying hours; we were just doing a major job of face lifting, and the results were still unknown. But even more to be respected were the mysteries of high-speed flight, engine failure, and altitude. The last two were inseparable; it would be bordering on suicide to go even 100 feet off the ground without first investigating how the ship would handle without power. We knew, theoretically, that the rotor should keep right on turning—but theory and practice sometimes need a little coercing to get together.

Nevertheless, instructions had been received, and we redoubled our efforts. On March 31, the ship was out again.

Autorotation—gliding without power—was uppermost in our flight schedule. It is a most interesting phenomenon and has been the subject of many learned treatises. A complete discussion of it could fill the whole of this book. However, it is not proposed to explain it fully here. Suffice it to say that a helicopter or Autogiro rotor in flight will keep turning without engine power if the pitch, or bite, of the rotor blades is not too great. The best pitch is between two and five degrees. Many people have the idea that, if the engine fails, the rotor first comes to a stop and then begins to windmill in the opposite direction. This is not correct. The rotor *continues* turning in the same direction, and at about the same speed, as if it were power-driven. It rotates by itself; that is, it "*auto*rotates."

Naturally, any heavier-than-air vehicle needs power to make a sustained flight. Therefore, the Autogiro and the helicopter, without power, must glide downward. But autorotation keeps the sinking speed within reasonable bounds, and the craft may be guided into any desired field. If needed, the descent may be straight down, or even backward or sideways, but autorotation continues under all these conditions.

So much for the simple facts of autorotation. It was of paramount importance for us to make certain that the XR-4 would conform to these requirements. So on April 3 I flew "cross-country" for a quarter of a mile from our little meadow to the airport. There, over the long paved runways where an emergency landing might be made at any time, I would try to approach the power-off condition. In normal powered flight, the pitch of our blades was about eleven degrees. For autorotation, something less than five degrees was required. This meant that the pitch lever would have to be lowered through the intervening range, and the craft would therefore be settling toward the ground.

We decided that the safest procedure would be to fly forty to fifty miles an hour, about 100 feet high. Pitch would be reduced as rapidly as possible, and when the ship was within twenty feet of the ground, a so-called *flare-out* would be made by tilting rearward and slowing down the ship. We could tell when we had reached autorotation by watching the tachometers that showed engine and rotor speed. When the rotor tachometer indicated more speed than the engine, it would be obvious that the engine was no longer driving— and autorotation would be achieved.

These tests were the most difficult of any I have ever done. Active coordination of the throttle was required as pitch was quickly reduced. The rudder had to be readjusted because of the changing power applied to the main rotor. I had to watch the air-speed indicator (to be sure I wasn't slowing down or speeding up), glance at the pitch indicator (to see how close it was to five degrees), keep an eye on the two tachometers (for signs of autorotation), and watch the ground. I was glad I had once taken lessons on a pipe organ—they certainly came in handy now!

THE AUTHOR PILOTS THE XR-4 FOR ITS FIRST FLIGHT.

THE COMPLETED XR-4 DEMONSTRATES A USEFUL QUALITY.

THE FIRST HELICOPTER FORMATION FLIGHTS IN HISTORY WERE MADE WITH MR. SIKORSKY AS THE PILOT OF THE VS-300 AND THE AUTHOR FLYING THE XR-4.

Several attempts were made this first day, but the results were inconclusive. Their primary value was in the training I received, and I couldn't concentrate so hard for more than a few minutes at a time. Therefore we interspersed these flights with some speed runs. We had reason to believe that our air-speed indicator was not entirely accurate, so we had a car pace the craft to check it.

It was then, for the first time, that we began to realize how quickly a helicopter can get moving. I would hover close to the car, and at a given signal we would both start away. The car was noted for plenty of power and pep, but invariably I would find myself far in front without making an effort. In fact, it was an effort to hold down, so as not to spoil the trials by leaving the car too far behind.

Since then, actual acceleration tests have demonstrated that the helicopter can pick up or stop more quickly than a car. From a hovering start, sixty miles an hour can be reached in 200 feet—and an average stop from sixty requires only about 125 feet.

The most interesting part of all this is the total absence of the things that you usually associate with quick stops and starts in a car. There are no squealing tires—no sudden neck-stretching lurches. You are not thrown forward or backward in your seat. Instead, the seat tilts comfortably under you at all times, very much like a child's swing. You know how pleasant it is to ride in a car around a well-banked curve; in the helicopter, not only the curves are banked, but all the starts and stops are, too.

However, this doesn't get us along with the power-off test flights at the airport early in April. The second day of trials, I was able to secure actual autorotation by starting about 200 feet high and employing the technique I had developed during the many earlier attempts. The glide, with the engine slightly throttled, was quite pleasant, and it was obvious that the ship lost no part of its excellent control. We were greatly relieved, too, that the change from powered flight to autorotation, and vice versa, was free from transitional vibrations. The completion of this test marked the casting aside of our last fetters—we could now feel free to fly at higher altitudes without fear of serious trouble if the engine should fail.

A few days later, Gregory (Lieutenant Colonel by now) dropped in to arrange final details of the official demonstration. I took him for his first ride in the XR-4, and he spent more than twenty minutes flying it himself, handling the controls, getting the "feel" of it.

Finally I shouted, "I'll show you a power-off glide." He nodded his head and watched intently as I climbed to 300 feet above the airport, then lowered the pitch lever to three degrees, and throttled back. We glided down smoothly, and a broad grin lit his face as I banked slightly to one side and to the other.

"I think I'll land her," I said, when we were about 100 feet high. I had never before actually landed a helicopter without power, but everything felt so "right" that it seemed quite natural to carry it through.

"Okay," he smiled. At about twenty feet I eased back slightly on the control stick to sense its effectiveness so that I would be prepared for proper timing in the flare-out. Everything was as I would have expected, so I continued the glide to within five feet of the ground, then moved the stick backward again at the same moment that Gregory gave instinctive endorsement by visibly pressing backward in his seat. The glide decreased, the ship flared out as it tilted rearward, and we settled softly onto the runway. The tail wheel touched first, and the ship rocked forward onto the main landing gear, then rolled about ten feet to a stop. Our first power-off landing was a definite success.

We concluded the day with some load-lifting trials, in order to be prepared for the coming demonstration. Theories and counter-theories had been expounded for many years on a helicopter's ability (or lack of it) to carry appreciable loads. We decided there was no better time than the present to find out something practical on the subject.

We had two men stand, one on each side of the landing gear, and I took off and hovered with them. It seemed so easy that we put another man in the passenger seat (making four people, including myself) and hovered again. If the men clinging to the outside had been firmly secured, it would have been possible to fly away with them, because, once the ship had begun to move, it would have picked up extra lift from forward flight. We were more than gratified with our findings—particularly since it is a standard rule of aviation that an experimental airplane is invariably 10 to 20 per cent heavier than planned—and the XR-4 was no exception. If we should redesign it to save even 10 per cent of its weight, we could carry another man with equal ease.

Gregory openly expressed his satisfaction with the craft's flying qualities and was especially impressed (as, indeed, were we all) by the power-off landing and the load-carrying pos-sibilities. His outspoken encouragement was a much-needed stimulus to the effort ahead.

The following day, all aerial traffic was grounded by weather. The cloud ceiling varied from 200 to 500 feet, and there was moderate to heavy snow. Nevertheless we felt we could learn much by continuing our flights, so we received special clearance from the control tower and went to work.

It was interesting, flying in the snowstorm. Gregory and I occasionally were right up in the cloud base, so that the ground would fade almost out of sight. We kept the side windows open, because the snow built up quite solidly on the front and we had to fly by watching around the corner.

We were safe from other traffic, of course; but we found one point that may be of use at some future time when helicopters become more plentiful. I could see quite well if I turned the ship slightly sideways and flew crab fashion—a maneuver not recommended in a snow-covered automobile!

The next ten days were busy ones. We still had much to learn before the Army board arrived on the twentieth. Also, as a precaution against bad weather canceling the demonstration, we took moving pictures of the ship performing all its "normal" maneuvers, as well as engaging in many staged tricks to prove its controllability. These films would be used if we had to call off the actual flights.

One of the tricks was the first discharging of a passenger from an aircraft in free flight—at least, the first one in which the passenger survived without the aid of a parachute. I hovered three or four feet above the ground while my companion jumped out. It was interesting from two standpoints. First, it demonstrated a practical method of dropping people where even a helicopter might be unable to land (a quality that was more recently put to good use in rescuing a company rowboat from the marshes where it had been carried by a storm). Second, it showed the controllability and steadiness of the ship. When the man's weight suddenly left the front, right-hand side, we might expect a severe unbalancing effect leftward and to the rear, as well as a pronounced ascent of the entire craft. Needless to say, all these tendencies were present, but it was a simple matter to compensate for them with a very slight movement of the controls, so that the net result was hardly more perceptible than when a person jumps off the running board of a car.

Another even more practical trick was the use of a rope ladder for taking on and discharging passengers. We attached the ladder to the side of the ship and Ralph Alex volunteered to try it. It was surprising how easy it was to hover twenty feet in the air while his weight swung around below. In fact, I found it difficult to be sure when he was down, because I couldn't see the end of the ladder, which was hung from the opposite side of the fuselage, and I couldn't feel any appreciable change as he stepped off. This rope-ladder idea may have many ramifications in lifesaving, including the transportation of doctors or workers into restricted areas where trees or other obstacles might prevent a landing and also the lowering or raising of life rafts, materials, tools, food, and medicine.

For quick discharging of people from the craft, we found that a plain dangling rope was quite satisfactory. This trick intrigued Mr. Sikorsky, and he announced that he wanted to do it. I had great confidence in his physical ability, but I couldn't help wondering what would be the status of the pilot if Mr. Sikorsky's foot should falter when he was hanging underneath. I hovered at about ten feet first—but he signaled me higher. I tried twelve feet, and he still wasn't satisfied. We ended twenty-five feet high—and I believe he really was sorry the rope wasn't longer!

As he sat in the door, just before dropping over the edge, I would have sold my job to the first bidder. It was a tremendous relief when I received the signal that he was clear—and safe.

Still another practical demonstration was an actual two-way telephone conversation between my passenger and a person on the ground. Captive balloons and airplanes have been used for controlling gunfire by reporting to the gun crew where their shells were falling. But balloons are clumsy, inflexible targets for the enemy; and reporting by radio from an airplane may not be satisfactory owing to interception or interference, and also owing to the fact that it must be always moving. The helicopter, however, could provide telephone contact from a stationary vantage point, while still maintaining flexibility in an emergency.

One series of flights was made to record what was, to the best of our knowledge, the first formation helicopter flying in history—in fact it was perhaps the first time two helicopters had ever been in the air together. Mr. Sikorsky piloted the VS-300, and I flew the XR-4. We took off, hovered, and landed in formation and made a number of trips out over the marshes and back across the meadow.

But movies were not our only job during these days. We ran some full-speed tests and found that the top speed of the XR-4 was in the neighborhood of eighty-two miles an hour. I was deeply sorry that wartime restrictions prevented us from officially going after the world speed record for helicopters established by the German FW-61. The most I could do was to chalk up another "unofficial" to my credit.

We made some power climbs, also, to check the rate of climb against our calculations. Altitude records were made and broken every few minutes, finally remaining, for a while, at 2,000 feet.

We had a total of only 9½ hours in the air, but our experiences had lightly touched pretty much the entire range of helicopter operation. It had been sketchy, had not delved deeply into the many, many problems that we knew were there, but it had given us the information and the confidence we needed, so we put the ship in the hangar for careful inspection to be in readiness for the Army demonstration.

It was a cold April 20. The sky was gloomy and overcast; the wind was moderately strong with gusts that often shook down some light rain. Nevertheless, we decided to fly, and late in the morning we escorted our guests to the meadow behind the plant. Most of them were U. S. Army officers, but Great Britain was represented, and two or three civilian agencies of our government.

On the whole, the group could not be called enthusiastic. Interested, yes; skeptical, perhaps; courteous and open-minded, definitely. But not enthusiastic. They studied the details of the machine, listened carefully to the explanation of its controls. But they didn't get excited about it. There was a conspicuous Missouri-ness in their attitude.

After the preliminaries were over, I stepped into the cabin with the outline of the carefully scheduled program in my pocket. The ship was sitting in the center of a twenty-foot square marked on the ground. Most of the landings and take-offs were to be made with the wheels inside that area. The main wheels were ten feet apart, and it was twelve feet from the main wheels to the tail wheel, so the margin was only four or five feet. To the uninitiated, it would be impressive; to us, it was routine.

I took off, hovered, flew over the fence, and landed in the paved lot beside the factory building; then flew backward to a very small fenced-in enclosure and settled down amongst a mass of old jigs and fixtures; then returned to the marked square and landed.

Next came a demonstration of forward, backward, and sideways flight, and slow twisting flight at low altitude between rows of trees.

Then, starting from the square, I took off and climbed absolutely vertically to 500 feet, following this with fast flight two or three hundred feet high, including steep turns, and ending with a power-off glide.

A quick start was demonstrated, and we repeated our old VS-300 stand-by of spearing the ring with the nose of the craft. Then Alex climbed up the rope ladder, pulled it in after him and we flew away, returning shortly for him to climb down again.

We came in and hovered while someone on the ground handed my passenger a parcel. We demonstrated descent by a single rope, telephone communication, and the passenger jumping out in flight.

Then came a novelty act. We had a dozen eggs in a net fastened to the ship by a long rope. I took off, lifting the eggs high in the air. When they had stopped swinging, I lowered them gently back onto the ground and the witnesses were called to observe that not one was broken. Labensky cracked one to prove they were not hard-boiled!

We demonstrated load lifting by again carrying four men off the ground.

Finally came the climax. I donned a parachute and took off for altitude. The solid cloud base was probably 10,000 feet high, and I had no intention of reaching that. But scattered puffs of rain clouds hung as low as 3,000 feet, so I headed between them and climbed straight into the wind. The only thing that troubled me was an occasional sprinkle, and since the temperature was close to freezing, I wondered whether the blades would start to ice up. We had had no experience with icing, so I watched carefully for any roughness or power loss that might indicate trouble.

Up past 2,000, 3,000, 4,000. I was aiming at Gregory's request, and since the machine was functioning well, I kept on until the altimeter crossed the 5,000-foot mark. This not only fulfilled his wishes, but also set a substantial—if unofficial—American altitude record for helicopters.

It would have been unwise to go higher. The clouds were closing in around me; and furthermore, some investigation of the flying characteristics at this altitude would be advisable before pressing on. So I eased down on the pitch-control lever. Immediately a strange series of events took place. The craft began to shake quite sharply; it swung around in a half-circle and seemed to be almost out of control. For several quick seconds, I hung onto the stick, wondering what had gone wrong and what to do about it. The comforting thought of the parachute flashed through my mind as I instinctively held the control stick forward to "keep flying speed." Apparently this unconscious action did the trick, and in a few seconds I found myself in a normal power glide.

I came down to 2,000 feet under part power; then made a power-off descent to the ground and the demonstration was concluded. No one there knew what I had experienced at 5,000 feet; and, aside from that one episode, the program had been an outstanding success.

Enthusiasm of the guests had begun to bud during the early part of the program. It had blossomed out noticeably as each demonstration proved a new and interesting point. At the end, it was in full bloom. There remained no question in the mind of anyone there that the XR-4 was a flyable craft. Granted that it had shortcomings in appearance, power, speed—still it could do a job of work even in its present condition. And everyone realized that this was only a start—comparable perhaps to the automobile of 1910.

The Sikorsky helicopter had come through its official debut with flying colors.

Only one question remained in my mind: What happened at 5,000 feet? Later on, I reproduced the difficulty and discovered that it was purely a piloting error involving loss of air speed coupled with over-speeding of the engine. It was the result of inexperience amplified by the loss of ground reference at that height.

# Chapter IX

## HISTORY IN THE MAKING

AFTER THE PARTY WAS OVER AND THE GUESTS HAD DE-parted, Gregory was like a kid with a half-empty bowl of ice cream still sitting on the table. He hurried back to the XR-4, and I took him up for some more instruction.

The following day we tackled it again, and it soon became obvious that I was no longer needed on board. I hadn't touched the controls for some time, and I had long since run out of things to explain.

So I turned to him and said, "You're doing all right. Go ahead and take it up solo."

Amid his good-natured remonstrances, I stepped out and left him to his own devices. Carefully he felt his way through the problem as he eased the ship off the ground, seeking the proper position for balance now that my weight was no longer there. As I watched him flying the XR-4 alone—as I had my first opportunity to stand on the ground and observe it in the air—I felt like a father who had just given his daughter in marriage. I was happy, but jealous—and I wondered if he would take care of her as I had tried to.

From this day on, we directed our entire attention toward accomplishing the second part of Gregory's instructions—the delivery flight to Wright Field. Much remained to be investigated. We had not yet flown for even one continuous hour, and there were a hundred little items that still needed attention. So for the first eleven days in May, we put in more than five hours in the air. On the eighth I made the first true cross-country helicopter flights in America by going from Stratford to West Haven and return—a distance of twelve miles each way! I made the round trip three or four times, staying up over an hour and getting used to the strange sensation of "going somewhere" again. For a full year, my flying had been entirely within a one-mile radius of my point of take-off, and, although I knew every bush and grass blade in that area, I had almost forgotten what the rest of the world looked like from above.

Finally it was settled that I would leave for Dayton on Tuesday, May 13. So on the preceding Sunday we made the last few tests and then turned the ship over to Plenefisch and his crew for final preparation.

Tuesday was a beautiful warm day, with the temperature close to 80° and a gentle breeze barely stirring the stately elms that bordered our little field.

I sat inside the blunt-nosed cabin, reading the instruments that would tell me when all was ready, arranging maps and parachute harness, watching the rotor flicking overhead in powerful rhythm. Several of my friends drifted out of the crowd and stuck a farewell hand in the open window.

Mr. Sikorsky hovered near, nervously chewing at the corner of his mouth. His keen gray-blue eyes flashed out from under the familiar gray fedora as they searched every detail of the craft to detect any sign of flaw. I knew the capacity of those eyes from experience—that time they had seen from twenty-five feet the strut that was so slightly bent that I had to sight along it at close range to notice it—the time when, without apparently looking at the ship at all, he had commented on a tail-rotor blade whose tip had an eighth-of-an-inch nick in it. And I knew on this May morning that his vision would be doubly sharp because he was not wholly convinced of the wisdom of the impending flight—he felt that this "first-of-the-type" should be handled with kid gloves and should be delivered to Dayton by truck, thus eliminating the potential hazards of a cross-country trip in a totally novel type of aircraft that had had less than twenty flying hours since its wheels first left the ground. So I knew those eyes would probe to the marrow any minute indication of things awry.

It is understandable, therefore, that I experienced a calm reassurance when he walked quickly to the ship, thrust out his hand, and said, "Well, Les, today you are making history!"

But I couldn't tell him what I wanted to: that I was only the ball carrier in a football play that was destined to be a brilliant touchdown. The play had been nurtured and studied in Coach Sikorsky's mind since 1909. It had profited enormously from similar plays worked out by other coaches throughout the world. The snap of the ball had found a stout engineering and shop team on the line and in the backfield—running the interference, taking the knocks, and clearing the way, so that now the lone ball carrier might trot across the goal line standing up!

The engine roared its crescendo as I pulled upward on the pitch lever. The ship lifted vertically to ten or fifteen feet; then I eased forward on the stick and started across the field. Sweeping in a gentle circle, I swooped low over the clump of upturned faces and waving hands—on over the factory and into an easy climb to 1,500 feet.

A car with a large yellow dot painted on the roof was already speeding out the factory gate—it was to be my shadow for five days. In it were the backfield that had been chosen to run the interference for this final play: Bob Labensky, the project engineer who had cast his lot with the penniless Sikorsky of nineteen years ago and had remained loyal through lean and rich alike; Ralph Alex, his assistant, who had labored endless days and nights to bring this craft to flying condition; Adolph Plenefisch, shop foreman on the helicopter ever since the first nerve-racking flights in 1939;

ROUTE OF XR-4 HELICOPTER DELIVERY FLIGHT, MAY 13-18, 1942.

and Ed Beatty, transportation chief, who elected to make this epic drive himself.

I quickly lost them in the elm tunnels of Stratford, but my maps were marked with the exact route they would take, so I followed it closely, always ready to land in some little field beside the road should the slightest thing seem wrong. They would see me as they drove by, and delays would be minimized.

Danbury was the halfway point on the first leg. It came in sight a little behind schedule. I was flying at 2,000 feet now, because the land was rising; and at that altitude there was a fifteen-mile head wind. Sixty miles an hour had been chosen as the best cruising air speed for the flight—easy on both ship and pilot—and the head wind cut my true ground speed down to forty-five.

The day was getting hotter, and the oil had been slowly warming up until it approached the danger zone. It passed 80 degrees (centigrade) and crept on up toward 85. It worried me, and I watched it so closely that I didn't realize until afterward that I was setting another one of those unofficial records—flying a helicopter across a state boundary for the first time.

Brewster, New York, drifted slowly behind and for a while my beacon was a winding ribbon of highway flanked on either side by almost unbroken forest. Finally, however, the open fields of the Hudson Valley caught my shadow like a giant whirling spider, and I began to let down for the landing at New Hackensack, just outside Poughkeepsie, thirty-five minutes behind schedule. It was pleasant to see George Lubben's shock of red hair come bounding from the hangar as I hove in sight. Lubben was at this first stop to give the ship a thorough going-over, and, as I came in range of the field, he had been talking by phone with the ground party, who had gotten as far as Brewster and called to check progress.

On this first leg, besides the crossing of the state line, another record was written into our logbook: the national airline-distance record for this type of craft was unofficially established at fifty miles (since no other helicopter in the Western Hemisphere had flown any appreciable distance before).

From New Hackensack, I swung north toward Albany, flying about 1,000 feet above the valley floor. The mounting heat was building great white thunderheads above the Catskills, but they were still adolescent and presented me with only a modicum of turbulent air as I passed in front of them. Just below Albany, a few tremendous raindrops spread saucers on the windshield, but that was the worst those ominous clouds could do.

At the airport, I decided to land on the line with the other parked airplanes, nosing the ship practically against the fence. This was something that no other aircraft would ever consider doing, and everyone rushed from the buildings, expecting me to pile up among the automobiles in the parking lot. But the landing, of course, was without incident, and as I walked toward the hangars someone in the crowd grinned, "What are you trying to do—scare the hell out of us?"

Another airline-distance record on this leg—seventy-eight miles.

From Albany to Utica was uneventful except for the pleasure of flying safely up the Mohawk Valley with the hills on either side often higher than the ship. I felt like the Wright brothers, looking down from my transparent perch two or three hundred feet above the housetops. Dooryards full of chickens and other farm animals would suddenly become uninhabited as hurried shelter was sought from this strange hawk—but the yard would quickly fill again as houses and barns ejected motley groups of human beings gaping skyward.

This trip was marked by constant astonishment, as people saw things happening in front of their eyes that they had never dreamed of before. This chronicle will be, in large measure, a report of their reactions and remarks.

At Utica I drifted up sideways in front of the hangar and hung there stationary for a minute or so while mouths dropped open wide enough to land in. Then I slid over to the ramp and squatted down. The guard greeted me as I walked up to the office: "I don't believe what I saw just now! Of course, I realize this is a secret ship, but do you mind if I look again when you take off?"

Mr. Sikorsky's World Endurance Record for helicopters

was exceeded on this leg: 1 hour, 55 minutes. Also, another four miles were added to my previous airline-distance record, bringing it up to eighty-two miles.

If it hadn't been for my constant concern over the mounting oil temperature, which now pushed close to 95 degrees centigrade, it would have been a beautiful flight from Utica to Syracuse. The sun was getting low in the west, the air was smooth, and a gentle tail wind puffed me into Syracuse Airport fifteen minutes ahead of schedule. As I hovered in front of the hangar where I thought we were going to house the ship, a guard burst around the corner to give me directions. His eyes popped open as he spread his jaws and his feet simultaneously, when he saw me awaiting instructions, fifteen feet up in the air! Recovered from his shock and reassured by my grin, he signaled me down to the other end of the field, and I could see apprehension oozing from the nape of his neck as he dogtrotted along the ramp with the helicopter's nose a few feet behind and above him!

This first day had gone according to schedule. The helicopter had for the first time in history proved itself an airworthy vehicle, capable of rendering true transportation. It had traveled 260 miles in 5 hours, 10 minutes without even beginning to approach its high speed. However, a quick inspection of the ship revealed one difficulty in this particular craft that was to give us our share of worry in the weeks to come: the transmission was heating up badly. It seemed strange that we should create a totally novel aircraft and run into no particular structural, functional, or control problems —while a simple gear transmission, something that had been developed and used successfully in hundreds of millions of applications during the last half century, was destined to hound our every move.

When we started for Rochester the following morning, I kept the ground party and their yellow-spotted car in sight

THE AUTHOR LANDING THE XR-4 ON THE RAMP AT WRIGHT FIELD.

THE END OF AN EPOCHAL FLIGHT. LEFT TO RIGHT: E. WALSH, A. PLENEFISCH, I. I. SIKORSKY, ORVILLE WRIGHT, R. P. ALEX, THE AUTHOR, AND B. P. LABENSKY.

LT. COL. H. F. GREGORY CONGRATULATES MR. SIKORSKY ON THE SUCCESSFUL COMPLETION OF THE XR-4's DELIVERY FLIGHT, WHILE MR. ORVILLE WRIGHT SMILES HIS APPROVAL.

BRIG. GEN. A. W. VANAMAN PRE-PARING TO BECOME THE FIRST GENERAL TO FLY IN A HELICOPTER.

for several miles, but finally decided to cruise ahead at normal speed. It was another beautiful day, but the hot, calm air presaged thunderstorms.

At the outskirts of Rochester, I noted that the main highway went straight ahead into the business district, while a small crossroad led directly to the airport a few miles away. I lingered, debating whether or not to hover there until our car came along and signal them the best route to take, but finally decided that, in the interests of the overheating transmission, it would be best to go on to the port and check things over.

Above the field, I headed into the wind and slowly settled down facing the open hangar doors. Several men working inside "ran for their lives," expecting a crash, but when they realized that there was no danger, they reappeared from behind airplane wings and packing boxes and watched the landing with unconcealed amazement. A guard came over and advised me to taxi up in front of the control tower at the other end of the hangar line. He didn't realize, of course, that a short flight in this strange craft was much more satisfactory than taxying on the ground, and he exhibited the usual reaction as I took off, still facing the hangar, and lazily buzzed along ten feet above the ramp.

The control tower was simply a square glassed-in box atop a fifty-foot skeleton tower at the edge of the operations area. No ship may land without first receiving a green-light signal from the control-tower operator. It was fortunate indeed that my ship could hang motionless in the air, because, when I whirred up in front of the tower and looked the operator in the face, he was so astounded that he completely neglected his duty and left me hovering there for the better part of a minute before he stopped rubbing his eyes. Then, with a broad grin, he flashed on the green light, and I settled to a landing at the base of the tower.

As I walked across the field, one of the instructors hailed me. "How do you expect us," he asked, "to train our students? Here we spend months teaching them to keep plenty of speed at all times—and then you come along and make liars out of us with that crazy contraption." (Confidentially, the next question that followed close upon this belligerent broadside was, "How soon can I get one of 'em?")

The transmission was still running pretty hot, so we decided to fly to Buffalo with the metal cowling removed from the sides of the ship to try to get more air circulation. With a head wind and a promise of thunderstorms, I stuck close to the ground party so that if an intermediate landing were required they would be able to check the gear-case temperature immediately.

Down the highway we went together. I knew they were pushing along at good speed (they said later that it was often close to seventy-five miles an hour), and I was hoping a state trooper would pull them over, so I could hover just beyond his reach while he was bawling them out, or even giving them a ticket. No trooper showed up, however, so I had to content myself with flitting ahead to each crossroad to make sure there was no converging traffic to cause danger: then signaling them to proceed without worry at the intersection.

As we approached Batavia the sky to the west became darker, and an occasional streak of lightning sliced down through the black curtain a few miles away. I edged northerly for a time to see if I could get around the storm, but it was spreading across my path. It looked pretty good to the south, but I hesitated to get too far off course, particularly since I didn't know what sort of conditions prevailed behind the storm front. So I finally decided to land and sit it out.

The car with its yellow dot had gotten itself misplaced somewhere in Batavia's traffic, and I wasn't sure which of two parallel roads it would follow toward Buffalo. So I leisurely swung back and forth between the two highways, trying to spot my earth-borne companions—keeping a weather eye on the progress of the storm in the meantime, and picking out a likely looking house with a telephone (I could see the lead-in lines from the road) where I could land and report my position. (Strange that with this aircraft neither the size of the available landing field, nor its surface conditions, had any influence on where to land, the only factors being a comfortable house and a telephone!)

For reasons I cannot understand, I failed to pick up the yellow dot on the highway (they claimed I flew directly over them several times), and after five or ten minutes the storm was close at hand. I swung in over the spot I had chosen—a nice green strip of grass about seventy-five feet wide between two ploughed gardens. On one side of the gardens was a comfortable old farmhouse with its unpainted barns rambling out from under the big maples. At the other side of the gardens stood a shiny new bungalow that looked as though it might originally have been one of the cozy family group around the farmhouse, recently become independent and gone modern.

As I came to a stop twenty-five feet above the green turf, that old bugaboo lack of power became all too apparent. The engine just wasn't able to cope with such unfavorable conditions as the calm humid air before a thunderstorm, and the "bottom" seemed to drop from under me. As the craft settled rapidly to earth, I spent a few uncomfortable seconds wondering about the safety of this experimental baby. Even here, the pilot's safety was not in jeopardy, because of the ship's unique abilities. The landing was a great deal harder than normal, but a quick check showed the machine to be unscathed by its experience.

The occupants of the house were only too glad to let me use their telephone. The owner—in his late seventies and on crutches—had been out in the chicken house when I settled in for the landing and was full of suggestions as to what had gone wrong with the engine, because he had heard it "sputter and backfire" when I came over. I don't believe he ever became quite convinced that the landing was intentional.

The daughter lived with her husband and eleven-year-old girl in the new offshoot of the family mansion across the gardens. "Is there anything I can do?" she asked, as I approached.

"Thanks very much," I replied. "I hate to ask you to stay off your own property, but we are under strict orders to let no one near the ship. Would you mind just keeping people away while I telephone?"

"Willingly," she said. So willingly in fact that, when Labensky and the others arrived during my absence, she firmly refused to let them pass until I had identified them.

After the storm was over and we were preparing to leave again, one of the people warned me quite persistently of a hidden ditch about 200 feet from the ship. I couldn't make him believe that I would take off straight up, so I finally quieted his fears by assuring him, with thanks, that I would be careful. The ground party reported that after the take-off his astonishment knew no bounds—that the eleven-year-old girl gasped momentarily, but quickly recovered and jumped up and down shouting, "Boy! Will I have something to tell 'em in school tomorrow!"

Another storm was skirted before Buffalo, but finally the airport loomed out of the haze. The control-tower operator, I suppose, could not be expected to guess that the queer contrivance being visited upon him would not interfere in the slightest with an air liner that was about to land on the runway—so he gave me the red light. A short flight around the hangars brought me back to the tower a second time, and, although the air liner was still on the runway, the operator

realized I saw him and flashed the green signal for landing.
I settled in slowly over the buildings while a sea of faces
gaped upward. I purposely overshot the edge of the ramp
by twenty feet—then stopped and backed up onto it! The
ground party, on hand for the landing, drifted through the
crowd and heard:

"I never thought I'd live to see one *back up!*"

"I've given up drinking from now on!"

"Well—now I've seen it all!"

One of the younger mechanics made the error of taking
the story home to his family that night and gleefully reported
the next day that his father, in all seriousness, said, "Son, I
want you to give up aviation. When you start seeing things
like that, it's time to make a change!"

Owing to a long string of thunderstorms between Buffalo
and Cleveland, we canceled out for the day and made arrangements to store the ship under guard.

## Chapter X

## MISSION COMPLETED

THE FOLLOWING DAY WAS NOT AT ALL PROMISING. LOW clouds covered the lake shore, scattered showers were predicted, and there were head winds up to twenty miles an hour in the offing. We decided to take a shot at it, however, and got away late in the morning.

The usual weather prevailed in the pocket below Buffalo—very smoky, hazy conditions cut visibility to less than a mile—but I steered my course half by compass and half by highway in order to be close to the road the ground party was following.

Once, as a towering radio mast loomed out of the murk, I was vividly impressed with the value of an aircraft that could come to a complete stop in mid-air if necessary. How comforting it was to know that I didn't have to barge through this stuff at 80 to 100 miles an hour!

The lake shore finally came in view, and I followed it without incident to the government intermediate field at Dunkirk. The field was still wet from the storms of the night before, and the attendant was dumfounded when I hovered about until I found a high spot near the building where there were no puddles to step into.

The transmission was no better and no worse. I decided I could take one of the ground party on the next flight, and a flip of the coin chose Ralph Alex.

The weather was closing down so that, in any other aircraft, I would have been uneasy. Above us were low, nasty-looking clouds. Below were two parallel lines of puffy white ground fog that hung over the highways where the warm moist air from the pavements met the cooler air that was drifting in off the lake.

A few minutes after the take-off, we came on a bird about the size of a robin straying at our level. When he suddenly realized that an aerial meat grinder was fast bearing down on him, he fluttered a couple of times trying to decide which way to go—apparently couldn't make up his mind—and finally in desperation folded his wings and plummeted for the ground.

It was on this flight, in the middle of a driving rainstorm, that a helicopter passenger was carried for the first time across a state line (New York-Pennsylvania).

At Erie, weather forecasts were bad: high winds, lake storms (I knew from past experience what they could be), very low clouds, intermittent fog. The low clouds and inter- mittent fog bothered us only because we would be breaking Federal regulations if we flew through them without com- plying with instrument flight procedures (which we could not do for want of a radio). But the high winds, upwards of thirty to thirty-five miles per hour, we were not yet pre- pared to face—particularly if they were *head* winds as prom- ised. So we stowed away at Erie for the night.

The next day we took off at noon in the face of a twenty- to twenty-five-mile wind, because the forecast showed the probability of worse weather to come, which we might avoid if we got on to Cleveland.

A few minutes out of Erie, I realized that the transmission didn't sound the way it should, and I could occasionally feel through the rudder pedals a kind of catching, as though small particles of solid matter were getting crushed in the gear teeth. After a few minutes, it seemed the best policy to land and confer with the ground party.

When they arrived, it was decided that Labensky would

fly with me for a while to analyze the difficulty. If it were serious, we would land again—if not, we would proceed to our next scheduled stop: Perry, Ohio. It is significant that there never once entered into our deliberations the thought that we might not be able to find a suitable landing spot in case of trouble—with the helicopter, any tiny field was quite satisfactory.

For this whole flight, four ears were alert for untoward noises—and none appeared. Analysis some time later led us to believe that the extra passenger weight was sufficient to change the loading on the transmission so that it performed satisfactorily. Actually, however, it was slowly chewing itself to pieces and had to be replaced shortly after arrival at Dayton.

This was the roughest leg of the entire trip. The wind was gusty, varying from twelve to twenty-nine miles an hour. It was dead ahead, so I chose to fly low in order not to get into the stronger winds at higher altitudes which would slow us down even more. But close to the ground we got the full value of all ground "bumps." Whenever I saw a ravine ahead, I would brace myself for the turbulence that was sure to be over it. Every patch of woods had its own air currents; and to the leeward of a town or village the air was very choppy indeed. Many times we lost 75 to 100 feet of altitude in a down-gust—and we were only 300 feet above the ground most of the time. Once I watched the altimeter drop 180 of those precious 300 feet—and toward the end of the drop I began veering toward an open field, just in case it didn't stop.

But the ship behaved beautifully. It didn't pound and pitch like a conventional aircraft under similar conditions. All it did was float up and down and get kicked around sideways. There were no sudden shocks, and even when it yawed to one side or the other, it was not necessary to use the rudder to straighten it out—given a few seconds, it would come back by itself.

Labensky hadn't bothered to get a seat cushion when he climbed aboard at my roadside landing place. For 1 hour, 25 minutes he had been cramped up on a hard metal seat with the circulation cut off from both legs. After we landed at Perry Airport, he crumpled out of the ship, for all the world like a newborn calf trying to walk for the first time!

There was no gas at Perry, but we still had enough in the tank to reach Willoughby, where we refueled for the flight into Cleveland.

Although the weather was a little better, this was a troublesome section, because I didn't want to fly over congested areas quite yet. A long, sweeping circuit to the south carried me around the outskirts, and at last the Cleveland Airport loomed ahead. Somewhere down there, Mr. Sikorsky would be waiting. I learned later that he had picked me up with powerful binoculars eight miles away.

An air liner preceded me into the field, and I realized when I saw the green light from the control tower that they expected me to follow him in and land on the runway. But that was not the way of this craft; if I had landed out there, I would have had to take off again to get in to the hangars. My procedure was to fly down the hangar line until I discovered the one where storage had been arranged and then land on the ramp in front of it.

As I meandered fifty feet above the hangars, the green light followed me. I could almost hear the fellow in the tower saying: "Get that —— thing down!" He held the light until I drew close to the tower and then finally gave up. I hovered momentarily in front of him to see what he would do. He scratched his head—reached for the light again—thought better of it—and finally with both hands signaled me vigorously *down!*

I laughed and continued my perambulations. In front of one hangar there appeared to be more commotion than usual, so I headed that way. There was our crowd, Plenefisch and Walsh, and the hangar crew; and there, to one side, stood Mr. Sikorsky. He waved happily, and beamed with a broad, almost childish smile. A space had been cleared between the ships parked on the ramp, and I settled easily into it.

It was a thrill to shake hands again with Mr. Sikorsky. I wondered if the tears that flecked his cheeks were caused wholly by the wind.

The weatherman hadn't been very hopeful about the conditions from Cleveland to Dayton, but it turned out to be an ideal Sunday morning, with a gentle breeze and high puffy clouds.

Mr. Sikorsky joined me on this part of the trip, and after hovering for a minute or two in front of the hangar at Cleveland, we turned and started south while the ground party in the car was still getting under way. When we were on course, I turned the controls over to Mr. Sikorsky. It seemed strange for me to be telling him anything about flying a helicopter, but his duties had kept him so occupied that he had handled the controls of this Army machine only once, for two or three minutes at the plant. He quickly caught the feel of it— and from there to Mansfield I was simply navigator.

There was just one bit of advice that I repeatedly wanted to give him. He had learned to fly during the very early years of aviation, when everybody was reconciled to the fact that engine failure was synonymous with a crash—there was nothing you could do about it except rely on the resilience of the human body. On the other hand, I had been trained almost two decades later, when engine failures were still common enough to be a part of our daily diet, but something that we didn't need to take so stoically if we would simply keep one eye constantly focused on a suitable emergency field. Therefore, on this flight from Cleveland, when a large patch of woods loomed up in front of us, and we were only a couple of hundred feet above the topmost branches, his instincts and mine were sharply at variance. He would fly happily over the middle of the patch without batting an eyelash, while I would be gazing longingly at the open fields a half mile to one side or the other where we could just as well have been, at the expense of an extra ten seconds. For the first time in my flying career, I began to realize that woods are not a solid mat of tangled branches, as they had always appeared from my respectful distance, but simply a group of individual trees with a surprisingly large number of relatively clear spaces between.

Nevertheless, the clear spaces still looked terribly small as I peered down and mentally tried to fit our aircraft into them. So after two or three particularly large wooded areas had somehow nuzzled their way below our wheels, I basely abused my role as navigator. Whenever I spotted a forest looming ahead, I would point toward the fields to the right or left and say, "We're a little off course; we should be over there!" From the jagged route I made him follow, he must have thought me a highly incapable guide—but the remainder of the flight became very pleasant indeed!

Since he had never landed this ship, he handed the controls back to me as we approached Mansfield Airport. We landed close to the other ships, and he stepped out.

After a moment, he walked back. "Les," he said, "how are you going to get the ship over to the gas pump?" I looked at the row of airplanes deployed between our craft and the pump and sensed his suggestion.

"Well," I said, "if you will ask them to have someone hold the wings of the other ships, I'll fly over."

The clear space around the pump was about seventy-five

feet square, and a quick jump was all that was necessary. His happiness flourished in the ejaculations of the bystanders.

I took off alone for Springfield, because we thought it best to have the ship as light as possible. It was the longest flight of the trip—ninety-two miles airline. Furthermore, the day had become quite warm, and we were not at all sure of what was going on inside the transmission.

The miles slipped by uneventfully, and in due course the Springfield Airport was below me. A small training ship had just landed as I came over the edge of the field, and he began to taxi toward the hangar at the far end, unaware of my presence. I kept just behind him about five feet above the ground as he bounced slowly along. When he reached the ramp, he turned to line up with the other ships, then suddenly slammed on the brakes and stopped dead in his tracks. The pilot said afterwards, "When I saw you, I didn't know whether to open the door and bail out right there, or to give her the gun and try to take off over the wires!"

Before landing, I hovered a while, facing the incredulous group that emerged from the administration building. Then one young fellow signaled me very tentatively to move over slightly to the left. I obliged. With more confidence, he signaled me to the right, and once more I obeyed. With recklessness born of success, he signaled for me to go straight up in the air—and when I actually did so, he threw up his hands and quit!

"That's the biggest damn lie I ever saw!" he said.

While I waited for Mr. Sikorsky and the others, an Army airplane from Wright Field circled the port. In it was Lieutenant Colonel Gregory, who deserves a great deal of credit along with our group for the creation of this craft. Hard work, ridicule, high hopes, and bitter disappointments had been his lot for years while he and his associates tried to bring into being just such a ship. Now, at long last, the proof of their courage and foresight was here.

Gregory and I impatiently awaited the arrival of the ground party. When they finally showed up, the side cowlings that had been removed from around the gear case, to give better cooling on the trip, were quickly buttoned on for the dress parade to Wright Field. Gregory phoned that we would be in at three-forty, the engine was started, and Mr. Sikorsky took his seat again beside me.

Off we hopped with Gregory not far behind in the Army airplane and Labensky just behind him in another ship hurriedly chartered at the airport.

In fifteen minutes Patterson Field was below us, and as we looked over the top of a low hill, Wright Field came into view.

"There it is!" shouted Mr. Sikorsky. His face twitched just a little, and we exchanged another warm handclasp.

A couple of minutes later and we were circling the buildings. I couldn't resist the temptation to zoom low over the ramp once, just to show that we had arrived. Then we circled back and hovered in the space that had been cleared for us a few feet in front of the operations office. Mr. Sikorsky waved joyfully to the sizable welcoming group that had gathered.

We landed on a red-topped gasoline pit surrounded by airplanes of every description from the mammoth B-19 bomber to the tiny little private airplanes that were being considered for various military missions, and Mr. Sikorsky stepped out, proud and happy at the successful completion of an epochal mission.

Recapitulation of facts regarding the XR-4 delivery flight:
Five days elapsed time; 761 airline miles; 16 separate flights; 16 hours, 10 minutes actual flying time; four states covered;

first helicopter delivery flight completed; unofficial American airline-distance record repeatedly established and exceeded, finally to remain at ninety-two airline miles; first interstate helicopter flights (unofficial); first interstate helicopter *passenger* flights (also unofficial); World Endurance Record for helicopters exceeded with a flight of 1 hour, 50 minutes (most regretfully unofficial).

*Chapter XI*

## THE XR-4 GROWS UP

T HE SUMMER OF 1942 WAS A BUSY TIME FOR THE XR-4. There were a tremendous number of jobs to be done, and nearly all of them were wanted "yesterday."

They included: (1) complete performance tests to find out just what the ship could do in the way of speed, load, climb, descent, altitude, etc. (we had had time only to scratch the surface of these investigations before delivery); (2) preliminary operational trials, particularly bombing; (3) pilot training; (4) demonstrations to a multitude of persons ranging from the Secretary of War on down through generals and high-ranking officers, to official delegates from Allied countries; and (5), by no means least important, proving in practice the engineering and structural integrity of the Sikorsky helicopter.

The demonstrations began the day after we arrived at Dayton. Brig. Gen. A. W. Vanaman, Commanding General at Wright Field, naturally wanted to see the ship perform, and, judging from the crowd that gathered in front of Operations, nearly everyone else shared his desire. For this occasion, Mr. Orville Wright was on hand as a specially invited guest.

We had no time to give the craft more than a cursory inspection, so we kept our fingers crossed, particularly in the matter of the overheating transmission and the inherent shortage of power. It was a hot, sultry day with hardly a breath of air stirring; we had to fly from a sizzling concrete ramp instead of our accustomed cool grass; and the field was 800 feet

113

above sea level. Each of these factors would reduce our available lift by an appreciable amount; the cumulative effect of all three was definite cause for worry.

The demonstration itself went off quite satisfactorily, since we cut our gas load to the minimum and I flew solo. All the usual tricks were performed—I had come to feel like a trained elephant going through his repertoire. To top it off, Mr. Sikorsky held up his hat and I speared it with the nose of the craft. This seemed to be especially pleasing to Mr. Wright.

Then a few officers were scheduled for rides. Labensky and Alex sneaked around behind the ship and furtively felt the transmission. I could tell that they had burned their fingers, but they gave reluctant approval to make one more flight. When I landed, they surreptitiously investigated again and condoned another clearance.

One by one we took the passengers, each time hoping that the transmission would hold out. Finally came General Vanaman's turn. He is a large gentleman, and I wondered whether I could get off the ground with him at all. But, to make it worse, he was the commanding officer of the post and he felt obliged to conform to Army regulations, which meant wearing a parachute. If he wore one, I had to, too—and thus another forty pounds were added to the already laboring machine.

Labensky and I exchanged a quick glance. A slight shrug of his shoulders indicated that he wasn't giving any further guarantees, but that he thought it probably would last. So with my tongue in my cheek, I opened the throttle wide, struggled free of the ground, and staggered away. It was a recurrent source of amazement that when the XR-4 was really put to it she usually managed somehow to do the job.

Three days later, a major overhaul was finished and flying began in earnest. Gregory quickly brushed up his technique and spent intensive hours of training each day. A wooden

# ROSTER OF HELICOPTER PILOTS & STUDENTS

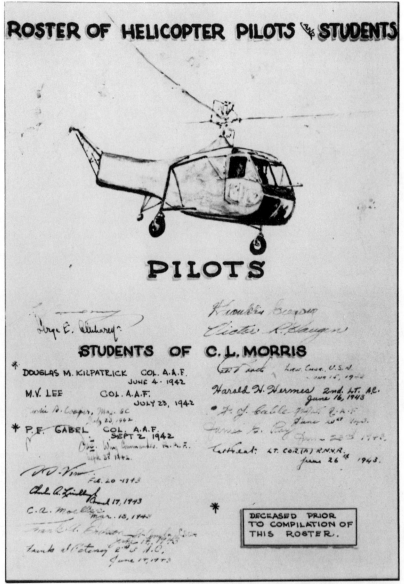

## PILOTS

## STUDENTS OF C. L. MORRIS

* DOUGLAS M. KILPATRICK    COL. A.A.F.
                          JUNE 4 · 1942

M. V. LEE            COL. A.A.F.
                     JULY 23, 1942

* P. E. GABEL        COL. A.A.F.
                     SEPT 2 1942

Harold H. Hermes    2nd LT. A.C.
                    June 16, 1943

* DECEASED PRIOR TO COMPILATION OF THIS ROSTER.

---

SIGNATURES OF THE FOUR PILOTS WHO PRECEDED THE AUTHOR: I. I. SIKORSKY,
SERGE E. GLUHAREFF, H. FRANKLIN GREGORY, AND VICTOR R. HAUGEN—AND OF
THOSE WHOM THE AUTHOR TAUGHT TO FLY THE HELICOPTER, INCLUDING DATE
OF SOLO: DOUGLAS M. KILPATRICK, M. V. LEE, LESLIE A. COOPER, P. E. GABEL,
R. A. C. BRIE, D. D. VINER, CHARLES A. LINDBERGH, C. A. MOELLER, FRANK A.
ERICKSON, FRANK W. PETERSON, C. T. BOOTH, HAROLD H. HERMES, F. J. CABLE,
JAMES G. RAY, AND E. A. H. PEAT.

ONE WAY TO RENDER AID WHERE EVEN THE HELICOPTER MAY BE UNABLE
TO LAND.

platform, twenty feet square, was constructed three feet off
the ground, so that simulated deck landings could be practiced. We could have used an area lined out on the ground
where missing the mark would be unimportant, but we felt
it would be far more satisfactory to the pilot and more convincing to the onlookers to realize that an error would mean
a crack-up. We made scores of successful landings on this
*deck*, and, perhaps I should add, no *unsuccessful* ones. In order to simulate as accurately as possible the conditions surrounding flights from small platforms on merchant vessels,
we set up a two-by-four *mast*, just beyond the tips of the
rotor blades. Even this very practical hazard didn't alter the
craft's ability to operate.

One of the most interesting projects was bombing. The
XR-4 had no bomb racks to begin with, so Gregory took
Col. Douglas M. Kilpatrick aloft with a twenty-pound
dummy bomb on his lap. Gregory would hover two or three
hundred feet high, and when he thought he was over the tar-
get, he would give Kilpatrick a poke and the bomb would be
heaved overboard.

After a while, I took a turn at it, and we developed quite
a competition to see which one could poke at the right time.
We became reasonably accurate, but we were surprised to
find how difficult it was to be sure we were looking straight
down.

Kilpatrick was my first real student. I couldn't take credit
for Gregory's training, because he had soloed the VS-300
long before I even entered the picture; but Kilpatrick was an
Army pilot with no rotary-wing experience, so I started with
him from scratch. He was the "guinea pig" on whom the
present helicopter student training curriculum was painfully
developed. He and I staggered through the air in the vicinity
of Wright Field for hours—he, trying to make the craft do
his bidding; I, trying to discover why he couldn't. His train-

ing brought to light most of the troubles that helicopter students must face, and the remedies for them. His limitless enthusiasm and his ability to smile in the face of adversity made him an excellent subject in this pioneering effort.

The first phase of the program was a brief introduction to the helicopter's controls. The control stick was quite sensitive, and the tendency of all beginners was to indulge in violent rocking, diving, and zooming for a while. Frequently, I would have to take over and straighten things out a few times before the student began to get the knack of it. This was a common difficulty, so that the onlookers and the crew became quite expert at judging, from the ship's antics, just when the newcomer had the controls. In order to give plenty of freedom for error, this stage of training was conducted at two or three hundred feet altitude and at moderate speeds.

Kilpatrick was an excellent pilot, but he was no exception to the overcontrol rule. However, after fifteen or twenty minutes he could hold her steady or make smooth turns; so he was introduced to the next phase, pitch and throttle, on which I had spent so many armchair hours before I made the first flights. In the XR-4, this was a particularly vital operation. If wrongly manipulated it could well be fatal. Most rotary-wing aircraft have no braces, struts, or cables to hold the main rotor blades from folding up. The only thing that prevents this is an invisible power as strong as any husky cable—and far more reliable—*viz.*, centrifugal force.

When you whirl a weight on a string, it is centrifugal force that makes it seemingly defy the laws of gravity, even to the point of being swung in a vertical path. The blades of a helicopter are acted upon by this same force. In fact, Mr. Sikorsky once said, "If we could find a rope that would keep its shape, we could use it for our blades—provided it would have the decency not to wrap itself around someone's neck when we stopped the engine."

But the centrifugal force of a given weight depends upon the speed at which it turns. If you were to swing a weight on a string quite slowly, it wouldn't stand out very far. The same is true of helicopter rotor blades. If for some reason the blades should gradually slow down in flight, they would be held out with less and less force. They would therefore "cone" upward more and more until ultimately they would fold up completely like an umbrella in a high wind.

For your post-war peace of mind, you should know that there are a number of ways to introduce a safety device against such an uncomfortable eventuality—and you can count on this matter being taken care of. One way is by means of an automatic-pitch-control device, so that as the blades cone higher their pitch automatically decreases, until it is low enough for them to start autorotating. As soon as that happens, they speed up again, and centrifugal force is restored in full. With such an arrangement, it would be impossible for the rotor ever to fold up.

However, in the XR-4, we had our share of mechanical difficulties from other sources, and we decided not to complicate the problem by trying any gadgets that were not absolutely necessary. We knew that, with proper training, it was safe to fly the craft without an automatic pitch device, simply warning all pilots not to let the rotor slow down below a certain safe turning speed. They were warned, also, that in case of engine failure the very first mandate was to decrease pitch instantly to the autorotative stage.

However, as I have already mentioned, the synchronization between pitch and throttle in the XR-4 was not perfect, and the pilot had to readjust throttle for each change in pitch. Since an error could be extremely serious, intensive and careful practice was the next phase of any student's training.

Several hundred feet in the air, Kilpatrick went through the process of moving the pitch lever slowly up and down, up and down, being certain to keep the rotor speed always above the safe minimum. It was hard work and plenty of it, but the idea gradually became firmly established. Then it was only a matter of a little practice to take over the whole job of handling all the controls in the air—stick and rudder, pitch and throttle.

With the fundamentals well in hand, we advanced to the hovering stage. The job was simplified by the air work we had already covered, but it gave me a certain self-satisfaction to find that Kilpatrick shared my early difficulty in trying to hold the craft accurately over one spot. It is a strangely slippery feeling, this hovering business. When you first start, it feels like trying to balance on top of a beach ball in the water. Of course, you have controls that the beach ball lacks, so after you have gained experience it becomes really quite simple.

When Kilpatrick's skill had developed to the point where he could keep the ship fairly close to a predetermined blade of grass and could land smoothly without drifting over the ground, I felt he would gain confidence if I were to send him up for a little solo practice in hovering.

I myself lacked experience as a helicopter instructor, and my haste to "turn him loose" was nearly disastrous, because one of the most troublesome things in handling the XR-4 was coming to a stop from forward flight. It required a great deal of coordination of all controls to do it properly, and I had not given Kilpatrick any instruction in this phase. It never occurred to me, when I stepped out of the ship and told him to "just take it up and hover a minute or two," that he might inadvertently start flying forward and not know how to stop.

All went well for his first flight. He took a few seconds to get accustomed to the ship without my weight in it, and then steadied down for some good hovering. After the landing, I signaled that it looked okay and he might try it again.

This time he began to creep slightly forward. He pulled back on the stick to stop it, but the ship climbed up a foot or two. This rather startled him, and, being a fixed-wing airplane pilot, he thought the best way to keep from climbing was to put the nose down and "dive." So he did, with the result that he picked up more speed and consequently more climb.

By now, I had begun to worry. I started dogtrotting after the ship in the 90° shadeless heat of Wright Field, mumbling to myself the instructions that I wished he could hear: "Drop your pitch, Doug!—no, not so much—keep up your rotor speed!—stop trying to land with throttle—back on the stick, now—that's fine—now up on the pitch—no, don't *over*control!" And so on all across the field.

Occasionally he would seem to be pretty well set, then something would happen and off we'd go again. After what seemed hours, but was probably not more than two or three minutes, he steadied down into good hovering, and gently got the machine back onto the ground.

As I panted up to the ship, he was shaking his head and wiping the perspiration from his face.

"What did I do wrong?" he grinned sheepishly.

"You did all right," I said. "You got it down whole, and you taught me a lesson: I'll never send another student up solo until he has learned to make transitions from forward flight into hovering."

In the next lesson, transitions were the order of the day. My own training in this phase had been gradually built up by the extensive starts and stops that comprised so much of our early testing. I didn't realize how troublesome it might be to someone who had not gone through that experience.

Transitions require coordination of all controls, if they are to be done smoothly. As the pilot approaches the point of intended landing, he pulls back slightly on the control stick and expects to stop. But the craft still has a certain amount of forward speed, so he finds himself zooming upward. To correct for this, he lowers the main pitch lever, simultaneously turning the throttle grip in order to keep the engine at proper speed. This changes the torque of the main rotor, and the ship begins to turn until a correction is made in the rudder-pedal position. Then, as the craft slows down and begins to settle, all those readjustments must be repeated in reverse order, *viz.*, increase pitch, adjust throttle, change rudder pedals back to their original setting, and push the control stick forward.

It is possible, of course, to follow those steps one at a time, as Kilpatrick did on his first solo, but this is a very jerky, unsteady procedure. To do it smoothly, they must be coordinated *before* their need becomes apparent in the antics of the machine. But I was still learning how to teach, and it took a great deal of main strength and awkwardness, coupled with superb stick-to-itiveness on Kilpatrick's part, to arrive, finally, at a sort of mutual understanding between himself and the ship.

From that point onward, it was smooth sailing. I am deeply grieved that a bomber crash put a tragic end to his career so that he cannot enjoy with us now the fruits of his willing labor.

On this matter of coordination, I was recently about to give an advanced check flight to one of my students with about fifteen solo hours in the ship. I asked him whether he had found anything that particularly troubled him.

"Yes," he replied, "when I am coming in to land and am just pulling to a stop in the air, the ship seems to take control and does all kinds of things that I don't assume any responsibility for! She rocks around and twists from side to side, and there doesn't seem to be much I can do about it."

A brief flight convinced me that he was not applying rudder at the same time that he increased pitch. This caused the ship to turn and rock sideways, and it took several seconds to straighten it out. As soon as the error was clarified for him, and he began to use rudder simultaneously, without waiting for the need to become apparent, the trouble disappeared.

One of the most difficult things for students to overcome is an instinctive, overpowering desire always to move forward. Pilots of conventional airplanes are taught to "keep flying speed"; they dare not slow down, especially when at low altitude. This is true to a certain extent even with Autogiro pilots, who have learned that, below a certain speed, the Autogiro must settle. Therefore a good deal of time is spent in forcing the helicopter student to hover over one spot. When a student had particular difficulty with this phase, I would often make him fly backward for long periods of time, on the theory that, once he had acquired this facility, he would then be quite satisfied to hover.

My first British student, Wing Comdr. R. A. C. Brie, Royal Air Force, was one such case. He found it hard to unlearn his extensive Autogiro experience. Even after he soloed, it was obviously a real effort for him. He would creep slowly forward at walking speed while I wandered along beside, trying to figure out how to stop him. At last I stepped out in front and held up my hand like a traffic cop. He approached, laughing, and pulled to an unsteady stop with the nose of the machine practically in my hand. Then I waved him back, and slowly, by fits and starts, he retreated.

Later on, when I decided to leave him to his own devices, he crept closer and closer to the fence and trees bordering the field. I could see him making a stupendous effort to back up, but he was still in open conflict with his Autogiro training. Finally he soared upward and over the trees, "doing an inadvertent circuit of the field," as he said later. Fortunately I had learned from Kilpatrick to teach every student transitions before solo, so he came through with a highly creditable approach, hovering, and landing.

It is quite probable that Brie shied away from backward flight because of an experience early in his training. He had the usual pilot's instinct to "get the tail down," when landing; but in the helicopter, if you get the tail down, you don't land. Quite the contrary. You take off—and backward!

Brie did that once. The more he pulled back on the stick, the faster we reversed—and the faster we reversed, the more he pulled back on the stick. We flew tail first, halfway across Wright Field, with Brie shouting, "I can't get the blasted thing down!"

It was with Maj. L. B. Cooper (now Lieutenant Colonel) that I had my worst troubles. They stemmed not from Cooper's piloting abilities but from his avoirdupois. Day after day, the XR-4 would gallantly strive to hover with his 230 pounds added to my weight—and day after day, temperatures of 95° with calm air would nullify its efforts. We finally let the wind indicator decide whether or not Cooper would get any instruction.

It was Cooper who effectively demonstrated the remarkable stability of our craft. We were flying around the field one day, and I signaled for him to take the controls. Then I rested my elbow on the window and dreamily watched the people below, while Cooper practiced making turns. After five or ten minutes he shouted, "Hey!" He was pointing at the rudder pedals. "Who is operating those?" he said. Neither of us had our feet on them, and yet his turns had been as satisfactory as could be desired!

That quality of the Sikorsky helicopter has become a

stock-in-trade. Every flight demonstration I give includes turns without rudder. Moving the stick to one side causes the ship to tilt toward that side, and the tilt is accompanied by an automatic turning. When the stick is neutralized, the craft straightens out positively and without "hunting." Quite steep banks, close to seventy degrees, can be made in this manner. Thus the rudder assumes minor importance in flight, and is used mostly for precision hovering—and of course for the inevitable torque compensation.

I had an opportunity at Wright Field to check out Capt. V. R. Haugen. He had flown the VS-300 in the early days of the Army's interest, but had not been closely associated with our more recent developments. He was one of my star pupils, soloing with less than three hours of instruction.

I have found that the average pilot requires between three and four hours' training before solo. A great deal of this time is spent forgetting the many practices and prejudices that he carries over from flying conventional airplanes—practices such as getting the tail down when landing—prejudices such as the aversion to slow speed and low altitude. From that point of view, I am led to believe that it may be easier to train nonpilots than to convert those who already know how to fly.

It is obvious, of course, that, once a skilled pilot has checked out on the helicopter, all his previous experience and "air sense"—meteorology, navigation, aerodynamics, coordination, knowledge of air currents and air traffic rules, and that indefinable "at-homeness" by which you can recognize a good pilot just as you can a good automobile driver—will be brought to bear. In this way, he will be ahead of a nonpilot who has accumulated the same number of helicopter hours but who lacks the background of air experience.

This is the reason why, up to the present time, only qualified airplane pilots have been trained on the helicopter: the military services have wanted to get the most out of these new craft in the shortest period of time. But it does not mean that only a qualified pilot is capable of mastering the helicopter; it simply means that, until now, no one else has been given the opportunity.

I believe that if two equally qualified individuals (twins, perhaps) were to begin flying from scratch, one in the helicopter and one in a conventional airplane, the helicopter twin would be soloing sooner, with more precision and more safety, than the other. Certainly, it is fundamentally easier and safer to be able to slow down, stop, and change your mind, than it is to have to plan far ahead how you will handle a two-ton mass approaching the ground at a minimum of sixty miles an hour.

This leads to a question that is often asked: "If I plan to own and fly a helicopter after the war, will it help to learn on a fixed-wing airplane now?" On the basis of the foregoing, the answer may be that the detailed knowledge you acquire in the relatively minor matter of manipulating the controls may be gained as readily in the helicopter as in a conventional airplane. But if you spend 100 hours or 1,000 hours flying an airplane now, you will be that much more capable of using a helicopter to its fullest advantage when the time comes.

A warning is in order here, too: the three or four hours of instruction before solo do not constitute the beginning and the end. They only bring the pilot to the point where he is safe to fly alone—but proficiency and accuracy have not even been touched. The next fifteen to twenty hours are spent pursuing a planned course that covers the whole list of things a helicopter pilot should be capable of doing:

Power-off glides (autorotation).

Turns over a spot.

Landings within six inches of a mark.

Hovering cross-wind and tail-into-the-wind.

"Jump" take-offs.

Quick starts and stops.

Hovering at higher altitudes.

Take-offs and landings both cross-wind and tail-into-the-wind.

Vertical descent from altitude without power or with part power.

Rough-air operation.

Many refinements and ramifications of the above.

Until he has mastered the foregoing, the helicopter pilot will not be capable of even backyard landings, much less the much-discussed roof-top landings that may come sometime in the more distant future.

But for those who may be disheartened by this thought, there is a reasonable hope of some improvement. We have thus far expended no effort in simplifying the helicopter's controls. We arrived at a solution that could be safely operated by two arms, two legs, and a brain; and immediately we reached that stage the Army wanted it. Simplification is easy and will come when time permits. In the interim, we accept whatever criticism may be forthcoming, believing that, under the urgency of war, we really haven't done too badly.

At Wright Field that summer, two other men received training: Col. M. V. Lee, who was doing a most excellent job of flying before he was transferred to another assignment; and Col. P. E. Gabel. Gabel arrived from Washington one morning about eleven o'clock on his way to the West Coast and announced that he wanted to learn to fly the helicopter before he left—at five o'clock that night!

"But that's impossible," we said. "For one thing, the ship is being overhauled. But even if that weren't so, it would take you more than a day to learn."

"All right," he replied, "I can arrange to stay through tomorrow. Just give me as much training as you can and I'll finish up later."

Next morning I began, and was astonished at the rapidity with which he learned. Before I realized it, he was ready to solo—with less than two hours of instruction. This was so out of line with my other students that I distrusted my own judgment and asked Gregory to give him a check ride before I turned him loose. Within a few minutes Gregory stepped out of the ship, and Gabel accomplished his wish.[1]

During this training period, the XR-4 passed another milestone—perhaps the most important one in its career. Heretofore, helicopters had been regarded as temperamental, delicate, and subject to endless troubles. They were an interesting experiment, but certainly not a recognized flying machine.

All those who had participated in our program realized that an accident of almost any nature in these early stages might set the entire development back on its heels, relegating it perhaps to a position of secondary importance in experimental work.

It was a great satisfaction, therefore, when official notice was accorded to the XR-4 on July 23, 1942, the day she passed the 100-hour mark. During those 100 hours in the air, she had broken trail for all the important performance factors in this type of aircraft; she had completed an epochal cross-country flight; and she had permitted five other pilots besides myself to secure basic helicopter training. This record was achieved in only six months and nine days from the time her wheels first left the ground.

From this day onward, no matter what might happen to the XR-4 or other models to follow, the helicopter as a type could no longer be disregarded. She had established a truly

[1] Gabel was killed in 1943 in a West Coast glider accident, before he had an opportunity further to apply his unusual talents to the helicopter.

phenomenal record that merited all the glory, both expressed and implied, in the following telegram:

DR. I. I. SIKORSKY, VOUGHT-SIKORSKY AIRCRAFT DIVN OF UNITED AIR-CRAFT; TODAY THE XR-4 PASSED THE ONE HUNDRED HOUR MARK AND COMPLETED THE PRIMARY TRAINING OF FIVE AIR FORCES OFFICERS TWO OF WHOM SOLOED THIS MORNING. FEW EXPERIMENTAL AIR-CRAFT HAVE ACCOMPLISHED SUCH A RECORD IN THE SHORT SPACE OF TWO MONTHS. I EXTEND MY SINCERE CONGRATULATIONS TO YOU AND THE MEMBERS OF YOUR ORGANIZATION WHO TOOK PART IN MAKING THIS POSSIBLE.

BRIG. GENERAL A. W. VANAMAN, WRIGHT FIELD, OHIO

## Chapter XII

## WORK AND PLAY

THE FIRST TWO ACTS OF THE DRAMA OF THE HELICOPTER were woven about the birth and development of the VS-300 and of the XR-4. The drawing of the curtain for the third act must await military authority. This chapter, then, is an interlude to present a few non-military highlights of our subsequent progress and to bring together some of the wartime developments that have been released to the public.

First, it should be made clear that the Sikorsky helicopter project has not stopped with the two models so far discussed. The XR-4 had hardly begun to show its possibilities before the Army Air Forces placed an order for some YR-4A's (Y means limited production quantity for service test; R-4, it is recalled, specifies the type; A indicates the first modification). But the XR-4's shortcomings were readily apparent, so in addition to the quantity order, two new experimental models were begun, in the expectation of achieving better performance, especially in speed and useful load.

During August, 1943, preliminary ground tests were made with the first of the new models to be finished: the XR-5. Her basic design had been formulated under the able project engineering of William E. Hunt, but when he left for another position, Edward F. Katzenberger brought her to successful completion.

On August 18, as I clambered up into the cabin, I wondered if everything would be in order for an initial flight. She was a mammoth craft for a helicopter—tall, heavy, with a 48-foot diameter rotor. The sound of the Pratt and Whitney 450-horsepower Wasp Jr. engine was awesome compared with the little Warners we had been flying before. The cabin, with its transparent molded plastic nose and sides, was as open as a greenhouse. It had provisions for two occupants in tandem, the pilot flying from the rear seat.

I cautiously started the rotor and went through all the preliminaries, just as I had with the XR-4 and the first YR-4A. Bit by bit I pulled upward on the main pitch lever and felt for those subtle indications that would tell if the controls were properly rigged; if the blades were correctly adjusted; if the engine, the landing gear, the tail rotor, and the transmission were functioning as they should.

At last the wheels cleared the ground for just a fleeting instant—then down again. I didn't have the stick in quite the right position, and I had started to drift sideways. But this brief experience had indicated a few simple adjustments that should be made before trying it again.

In the afternoon, she was ready for another attempt. As she lumbered into the air, I concentrated fiercely on making my responses conform with the totally new tempo of the XR-5's controls. Three times, I had to land momentarily to get a new start. But the fourth time, I was able to hold my own, and stayed aloft for about a minute.

It was a rough ride, that! The machine and I swayed, elephantlike, just off the ground—and, elephantlike, she picked up great clouds of dust from the newly graded flying field and spewed it over herself, her pilot, and the assembled company. But it was successful: the ship and I both survived.

From then on, progress was remarkably good. Performance figures and other details are yet to be released, but it may be said that the XR-5 has lived up to expectations and has proved herself a rugged, capable work horse.

In the early fall, the other experimental model was completed. Designated the XR-6, it was originally conceived as a cleaned-up version of the R-4 type, with a 250-horsepower Franklin engine supplying a good margin of power. As it took shape, however, the effort to save weight and to smooth out the boxlike contours of her predecessor resulted in a brand new machine.

She squatted close to the ground, and her long, cone-shaped tail stuck jauntily out behind so that she gave quite a cocky impression as I walked toward her on the morning of October 15, 1943, for the final ground tests. They were completed by noon, and in spite of a light rain, we decided to try a brief flight right after lunch.

The events leading up to the actual take-off followed the usual pattern: slow increasing of pitch and testing of controls, feeling for response and for neutral positions, listening for the overtones and undertones that mean so much, and at last breaking free of the ground. Then the usual quick analysis of conditions and adjustment to the craft's peculiarities.

Actually, the XR-6 was very much as we had expected. She responded briskly to the controls and had plenty of reserve power. But, as in the case of the XR-5, the most difficult part was getting used to the new noises. The XR-6 has a molded plastic cabin with soundproofing qualities. Also, the Franklin engine turns at high speed, humming very much like an overgrown sewing machine. The combination gave me a peculiar sensation of wondering whether or not the engine was really putting out power at all.

It was, of course. A 1-minute, 47-second flight proved it and started the craft on its way toward the months of re-work, readjustment, and tests that are the only known means of arriving at a satisfactory product. It was this work that made it possible for the XR-6, with Gregory as pilot and Alex, her project engineer, as passenger, to take off from Washington, D. C., on March 2, 1944, and fly non-stop to

THE AUTHOR FLIES THE XR-5, WITH BERNARD L. WHELAN, VICE-PRESIDENT OF UNITED AIRCRAFT CORPORATION AND GENERAL MANAGER OF SIKORSKY AIRCRAFT DIVISION, AS PASSENGER.

THE XR-6 IN AN EARLY TEST FLIGHT.

A FAVORITE DEMONSTRATION OF CONTROL.

A MUD LANDING. (NOTE TWO-BLADED MAIN ROTOR.)

HOVERING TO CHAT WITH A MAN "STRANDED" ON SOME SHIPPING BOXES. (NOTE TWO-BLADED MAIN ROTOR.)

THE AUTHOR LANDS ON A SMALL ROOF TOP.

SLOWING DOWN ABOVE THE YARD.

THE FIRST ACTUAL BACK-YARD LANDING IN HISTORY (SEE P. 139).

HOVERING.

LANDED!

Dayton, Ohio—a distance of 387 airline miles. They were in the air for 4 hours, 55 minutes, averaging close to eighty miles an hour ground speed, in spite of a ten- to thirty-mile head wind. Thus, several official records were unofficially eclipsed. It is now only a matter of someone deciding to do it, and all helicopter records could be brought to America by Sikorsky machines.

One of the greatest drawbacks of the written word is that it cannot adequately register the concurrency of events. Thus the reader may have gathered the impression that the VS-300 was a dormant or wholly forgotten project since the advent of the XR-4. This is totally erroneous. The VS-300's life was far from sedentary. She was engaged in innumerable investigations and demonstrations, as well as pictorial recordings of her prowess.

During one such flight, I had the opportunity to apply the helicopter in perhaps its first really useful role. Skimming over the Housatonic River one calm day, I noticed a small sailboat containing three disconsolate damsels in distress. The sail was hanging limp in the sultry air, and the current was carrying them slowly but inexorably toward the open waters of Long Island Sound. With a flash of inspiration, I circled down and hovered fifty yards off the stern quarter.

The damsels couldn't understand what was afoot, until my down-wash rippled across the water toward them and began to fill the sail. Then with obvious relish they hastened to trim away, and as I moved closer the little boat heeled over and plowed through the water, powered by my artificial but very effective wind. I stayed with them until they were safely beached, then waved farewell with a feeling of having done my good deed for the day.

This started us thinking, and we decided to record for public consideration a job of lifesaving that the helicopter might well perform. Mr. Sikorsky furnished an inflatable rubber boat, and we set up the cameras to film the first helicopter *sea rescue* in history.

One of our crew climbed into the boat and drifted out on the river. I took off in the VS-300 and dropped him a rope as I hovered overhead. Then I undertook to tow him to safety.

Unfortunately, safety was upwind and upcurrent—the wind was about twenty-five miles an hour, and the combination of current and ebb tide was running about eight. After I had towed awhile, I glanced ashore and realized that, contrary to expectations, I was drifting backward. So I tilted the machine ahead and picked up eight or ten miles an hour speed in relation to the land. This meant that the little rubber boat was going close to twenty miles an hour through the tide. It was a lot faster than it had been designed for, and it rebelled.

I couldn't see what happened, but the people on shore said it began to skim, first to one side, then to the other, with increasing sweeps until its nose dug into a wave and our luckless volunteer was summarily dunked at the end of the rope in the cold October water from which I was supposed to be saving him!

I don't need to report that the cameras stopped turning, because this was *not* the picture they had planned to take. The volunteer was dragged out by men in the company's "crash boat" that had been standing by—and, besides an unseasonal swim on company time, he suffered only the loss of his wallet containing his gasoline coupons (which the ration board later made good).

There was one thing on the VS-300 for which we always had to maintain a sharp lookout. Since she was intended only as a flying laboratory, there was a tendency to make any sort of test installation the quickest way possible, "just to see if it would work." We always told ourselves that, if we decided to keep it, we would spend time later to do the job properly—and usually we lived up to our intentions. Once in a while, though, we erred. It was this that led to my first—and only—potentially serious accident.

The design of our tail rotor had been worked out for the very early trials, when a limited amount of hovering was all that was intended. As we slowly pushed forward into full-fledged flying, however, the stresses at the inner ends of the tail rotor blades increased considerably. Nevertheless, we still had what Mr. Sikorsky would call a *toy* axle on the blades. It was not so husky as it should have been for the work it was now called upon to do.

We had a warning of trouble once, when Mr. Sikorsky himself was hovering. One tail rotor blade flew off, and the resulting unbalance twisted the structure so that the second blade hit the fuselage and disintegrated. Shorn of torque compensation, the craft began to turn around; but Mr. Sikorsky landed after a few seconds without further difficulty.

This was a warning; but we thought the failure had probably been due in large measure to weakness caused by a previous mishap when the tail rotor had struck the ground. So we repaired the damage without doing any redesign, and I told Mr. Sikorsky that I envied him his experience—the next time we had a tail-rotor failure, I wanted to be the pilot!

It wasn't many months before this facetious comment bore fruit. One cold March day, as I was making some pontoon flights over the river, I came on a flock of wild ducks. Most of them plunked headfirst to the bottom, their yellow feet flashing below the surface. But a few took to the air, and I decided to see if I could herd them in over the people on shore. I made a steep turn and had almost leveled out again when I heard a crack and the craft began to vibrate severely.

My first thought was that one of the main blades had hit

a duck, and I knew the safest thing was to land as promptly as possible. I decreased main pitch and applied hard rudder so as to head into the wind. But the ship didn't respond—in fact, torque made it swing in the opposite direction.

The next thing I knew, I was diving steeply toward the water, and only about twenty feet above it. I yanked back on the control stick and the pitch lever simultaneously. This apparently was the correct move, because we flared out and made a hard "splash" landing. The impact was sufficient to burst the fabric bottom of the fuselage and shower me with a large quantity of icy water, but otherwise the outcome might be termed generally successful.

Investigation revealed that one tail-rotor-blade axle had failed again and that the other blade had knocked itself to pieces on the fuselage. I had been properly repaid for my envious remark to Mr. Sikorsky.

We know now how to prevent such failures, and we wasted no time in strengthening the VS-300's axles. But I have berated myself ever since for not thinking fast enough to see how the helicopter could be handled without rudder control. We have always believed that, with an adequate amount of *keel area* at the tail, it would be possible to fly indefinitely if the tail rotor failed, so long as moderate forward speeds were maintained. Slight slipping to one side should supply enough torque compensation; and when the time came for a landing, it could be made in autorotation, since there would then be no torque to worry about.

However, I missed my opportunity to prove our theory in practice. The reasons were threefold: first, I had delayed for a split second, because of my snap judgment that the trouble stemmed from a *main* blade hitting a duck; second, I was turning when the blade broke, and the turn was in the direction of torque; hence the failure served to accentuate the turn; third, things happened much too fast! Forty feet isn't very high—and observers said that it was not more than four seconds between the failure and the landing. I had time for three distinct impressions: first, the vibration and my too-hasty analysis, second, reducing pitch to descend, third, diving at the water and pulling back on everything. That was all.

This anecdote leads to a question that has often been asked: What would happen if a helicopter's main rotor should hit a bird? The answer is: We don't know! That is one of the many things we haven't yet investigated. Inquiry among Autogiro pilots has failed to shed any conclusive light on the point. One says that he hit a bird once, and it didn't do any appreciable damage. Another says that the blade would certainly be severely damaged and the ship would shake violently.

We have no first-hand experience in the matter and therefore reserve judgment—quite frankly making every effort to avoid birds in the meantime. It might be added that the birds themselves appreciate our attitude and cooperate to the fullest degree. On countless occasions, I have played tag with gulls or ducks, and as long as I keep my distance they seem quite willing to stay in the game. They peer back over one wing or the other and flap harder and harder, until they look like a runner stretching for the tape at the end of the mile. But if I creep closer than forty or fifty feet, they give a couple of extra flips and double back under the ship in a tighter turn than we can possibly make, indicating a very keen distrust of the whole undertaking.

Occasionally, one will get caught in the down-wash of our blades and be blown into two or three somersaults. They always straighten out, however, and scurry off for a good long rest.

I'll never forget the time a tern was flying along beside me, about a hundred feet away. I began to bank toward him so that I would soon cut across his path. He gave me a couple of quick, worried glances, and finally decided he'd better do something right now! He reared up on his tail with his long, thin wings beating the air for all they were worth—I could almost hear the "tires and brakes squealing"! Then he high-tailed it in the other direction as fast as his weary pinions would carry him.

It may be said, therefore, that birds have no desire to mess around with the helicopter. Nevertheless, it is a very real problem that will require attention. Some day we shall probably borrow the "chicken gun" that is now employed to eject chickens at various parts of an airplane on the ground, to see what damage is caused. Then perhaps we can answer this question more adequately.

One of the early claims that we made for the helicopter was that fog would not interfere with its usefulness to any greater extent than it would with a car. It remained to demonstrate this in practice, however, and the opportunity came on March 17, 1942. The fog had rolled in off the Sound, and it was so thick that objects only a few hundred feet away were not visible. So we got out the VS-300 to record in moving pictures some actual fog flying.

It was a most interesting experience. Everything was fine as long as the old familiar landmarks were in sight—trees, buildings, roads. But when, after a little hovering, I had become mentally adjusted to the idea, I flew slowly off across the marshes until I could no longer see any such guides. Suddenly I became quite alarmed, not that I might hit anything— I was going too slowly for that—but simply that I might get lost out there and be unable to find my way back!

I crept along until at last a dark blotch loomed ahead. It was a tree, so I came to a stop and carefully looked it all over. What a relief! I recognized it! With confidence, then, I turned and headed in the direction I knew was home.

Since that first experience, I have made numerous flights

in fog—always at low altitude where I could still see the ground. Recently, the fog was so thick that, as I stepped out of the hangar, I had difficulty finding the helicopter at all, even though it was only a couple of hundred feet away. Nevertheless, after I had located it, the flights were made.

It should not be inferred that fog flying is something for novices yet. One of its greatest hazards comes from the almost invisible power lines, telephone lines, and radio antennas. A simple radio receiver might be developed to give adequate warning of their proximity. But for the present, it can be said only that the helicopter opens new and extremely interesting possibilities for operating in weather that, for conventional airplanes, is taboo.

One of our more interesting projects was the investigation of a two-bladed main rotor. For the greater part of the VS-300's life the main rotor had three blades. The XR-4 and subsequent ships are similarly equipped. But there have always been many tempting reasons for working toward a successful twin-bladed rotor. Two of the more obvious ones are simplified storage and simplified hub mechanisms. Storage would be excellent if the rotor could be stopped with the blades in line with the fuselage. Folding blades would no longer be required, thus eliminating not only a mechanical problem but also an operational nuisance.

The major drawback to a twin-bladed main rotor is the increased vibration it creates. Although the VS-300 was certainly flyable, it could not be considered wholly satisfactory, vibrationwise. We finally put the project in mothballs out of deference to other more pressing investigations of a wartime nature, but our encouraging experiences will keep it at the top of the list for post-war development.

We found that twin blades were able to do everything the three-bladed rotor could—plus. The "plus" was carrying two people in our little ninety-horsepower machine, which is something we had never before contemplated. Some of our best flying was recorded with this installation, and many of the photographs in this book that show recent "tricks" were taken during the twin-blade tests.

For example, landings and take-offs were repeatedly made on soft, sticky mud. With the pontoon undercarriage, we experienced no difficulty whatsoever. The weight of the machine was spread over such a wide area that it hardly left a mark. We had expected some trouble in breaking out of the mud to take off, but the only thing I ever noticed was a very slight rocking as one pontoon stuck a moment longer than the other. The instant the ship rocked, however, it freed itself, so the effect was only momentary.

Mr. Sikorsky has often made the statement that, with the pontoons, the helicopter can land almost anywhere, if there is room to swing the blades with a little margin for safety. He adds, "It can even land on ice; and if the ice is too thin and breaks, it will simply float on the water beneath."

We wanted to prove this statement photographically, so I landed one day on some ice that was much too thin to support a man. Unfortunately, the large area of the pontoons foiled us, because the ship wouldn't break through in spite of repeated hard landings. Finally I found a small hole in the ice and landed with one pontoon in it for the sake of getting the picture.

It was interesting to find that, on mud or ice, the ship could be taxied in much the same manner as on water. Moving forward, backward, sideways or turning on a spot could be readily accomplished, except that, in mud, more power was required and the movements were more sluggish.

In further efforts to prove the versatility of our machine, we operated from a great variety of outlandish and improbable places. One day, our "airport" would be some little salt creek or ditch, only four or five feet wider than the pontoons, with high banks on either side. The next day, it was a small boat anchorage, with the dredgings piled close beside it and jammed full of power craft. Then it was the sand pits. And finally, to cap the climax, it was atop a pile of empty aircraft-engine boxes, with gaping crevasses between them.

All these areas were perfectly practical landing places for the helicopter, although it was a little difficult to see any human need for transportation to many of them. Nevertheless, those experiences led to other more practical ideas.

With box-top training, for example, it was no trick at all to make the first helicopter roof-top landings in history. These were done on the company garage, probably 20 by 30 feet in size. With the experience I had gained in the creeks and inlets, settling in between closely parked cars presented no difficulty. And operating in and out of the boat anchorage trained me for what I consider the climax of the VS-300's and my career—true "backyard" landings.

We wanted some real backyard flights for the company film. It was decided that my own yard fitted perfectly Mr. Sikorsky's definition of a helicopter airport: "Just room enough to swing the blades, with a little margin for safety." The yard has four large trees, one in each corner. Smaller trees and shrubs, ten to twenty-five feet tall, fill in three sides, and the house itself effectively blocks the fourth, so that the landing could not be made except straight down.

The space between the overhanging branches of the large trees is about fifty-five feet across. The VS-300's rotor is thirty feet in diameter, and the tail sticks out another ten feet beyond. Therefore, assuming equal margin all the way around, the clearance was ten to fifteen feet.

As I circled over the yard, I began to wonder if the measurements had been properly taken. That little postage stamp between the trees certainly didn't look big enough to hold our ship. However, I decided to rely on our tape measure and came to a hovering stop at the topmost twigs of one of the large trees. Then, as the branches wildly gesticulated in protest, I settled slowly down onto the lawn.

Numerous landings and take-offs were made during the day. The craft was even maneuvered within the cramped quarters of the yard, turning this way and that for some particular pose. And after it was all over I was convinced—if I had ever needed convincing—that the helicopter would be my own future means of transportation.

It had been suggested that it might throw up too much dust to be a practical backyard vehicle, but actually the grass held the dust down very well. My family sat on the terrace and enjoyed the proceedings in complete comfort. In fact, the comfort lasted for several days while the mosquitoes that had been blown far away tried to find their way home again!

There are drawbacks, however. In my garden of tomorrow, I will not have larkspur, hollyhocks, and delphiniums. It took the flowers two weeks to straighten up from the down-wash of the rotor blades! (This is a tip to nurserymen: start now to develop oversized stems on your tall species. And a tip to future helicopter owners: plan to land on your roof, if you can—to preserve the garden!)

During one of the filming operations, I was flying over the river with a thermos bottle nestling in the VS-300's nose basket. It was the last flight before I would return to the field for gas. After I had completed the round, I discovered that the bottle had jounced out somewhere en route. There it was, floating merrily down the middle of the river. I flew out and tried to land on the water near it; but every time I approached, the down-wash would blow it away. Finally I succeeded in puffing it ashore; but this was hard on my waning gas supply, and as I flew into the field and was sliding sideways toward our fuel cans, the engine sputtered and stopped. I was only a few feet above the ground and moving sideways at a good clip, so I banked up sharply to stop the drift and settled down to a rather hard landing on one pontoon. The landing gear took the impact perfectly, and I chalked up my first engine failure in a helicopter.

During my association with the Sikorsky project, I have been privileged to give many important demonstrations, but one stands out clearly apart from the rest. It was a very brief flight for Miss Helen Keller, who, though deprived of sight and hearing throughout her entire life, "sees" more deeply and enjoys living more fully than almost anyone else I know.

Mr. Sikorsky had invited her to join us at the meadow in back of the plant, where the VS-300 would provide her with one more experience in her world of touch. Miss Keller has been up in an airplane many times; she even boasts that she flew one for more than half an hour. But since her knowledge comes entirely from touch, smell, or taste, she had never been able to observe flight in relation to the ground. Either she was on the ground, or she was in the air; but she could not stand on the ground and watch an airplane. The helicopter was her missing link.

Miss Polly Thomson, her companion and interpreter, deftly transmitted conversation by rapid finger signals in the palm of Miss Keller's hand. It was inspiring to watch her face as Mr. Sikorsky's explanation of the helicopter was relayed to her. She would nod her head, gasp in astonishment, or laugh heartily at some humorous idea. Finally she asked if she might touch the machine.

Guided by Mr. Sikorsky, she felt the nose structure, then the controls in the cockpit, and back to the landing gear. She was pouring out questions regarding the mechanical details and was obviously much interested in the central fuselage section, which contained the engine and the transmission. She followed the tail-rotor drive shaft out along the fuselage to the end.

Then she turned to Mr. Sikorsky and said, "Is it about thirty feet long?"

"No," he replied, "I think it's about thirty-five feet." One of the engineers corrected him. He chuckled and added, "You were closer than I was—it is twenty-eight feet long!"

The engine was started, and the breeze from the rotor blew on her face. The average person would have thought no more of it—there was a wind—that was all. But not Miss Keller. She stood and *felt* it, with all the senses at her command. It seemed as though she almost absorbed it through her pores, until she had built up her detailed mental images of what was going on.

Then a short piece of rope was tied to the VS-300's nose, and Miss Keller held the other end while I gently lifted the ship off the ground. Her expression was intense as she pulled lightly on the rope and felt the craft rising and settling, drifting to one side or the other, moving toward her or backing away. She fired questions and eagerly held out her hand for the replies. Certainly she was drinking in this experience to the full. It was one more step in her quest for a broader understanding of this world she had never seen.

After it was over, she said, "It was so buoyant! I could feel the lifting force of the machine. It was in some ways like Dr. Alexander Graham Bell's kite."

Night flights in our craft are extremely interesting. I have never cared to fly a single-engined airplane after dark because I have been unable to overlook the possibility of engine failure. A forced landing at night in a conventional airplane is not to be taken lightly.

The helicopter changes this entire concept. It gives a feeling of being able to get down somehow even under unfavorable conditions. The machine, to be sure, might suffer some damage; nevertheless the occupants know that they stand a good chance of stepping out uninjured because there is no reason to approach the ground at high speeds. If vision is poor, the pilot may glide in slowly, and if an obstacle should loom ahead, he can veer to one side or pull to a quick stop, landing straight down if necessary for the last few feet.

Our night flights were never done with benefit of flood-lighting. We were quite content with the light of the moon, when it was up. Otherwise we were guided by whatever few lights were glowing through our wartime dim-out. On the ship itself we had only the little red, green, and white *position lights*, which of course wouldn't help us to find a landing spot.

For the future, a headlight would be quite practical if it could be adjusted—forward for normal flying, vertically downward for landing. Then night flying would be a real joy to anyone whose senses were at all alive to sheer fairy-land beauty.

Recently, a group of men representing several helicopter companies met to discuss flight rules. In the course of conversation, the point was brought out that helicopters should have distinctive lighting at night, and it was tentatively suggested that we might mount colored globes in the tips of our rotor blades, thus making a multicolored circle. Distinctive, to say the least! The beauty of many a night would be truly enhanced by these Christmas wreaths whirling overhead.

There seems to be almost universal agreement that the advent of the helicopter will demand a broad revision in flight rules as a whole. Present regulations are almost entirely dictated by the airplane's greatest shortcoming—the fact that it cannot slow down or stop in the air. Since it must approach the ground at speeds faster than the average person cares to drive his car, the pilot's thoughts and reactions must be tuned to this unaccustomed pace, and his physical condition cannot be faulty. Furthermore, large areas must be provided for landing and taking off, and it is not always possible to have such areas readily available when trouble develops.

But, most important of all, traffic rules must be designed to handle an ever-moving vehicle. If, when you started out the driveway in your car, you knew that you couldn't go slower than, say, fifty miles an hour until you reached someone else's driveway fifteen or twenty miles away, you might be a hardy enough soul to undertake it, but you would certainly appreciate an omnipresent voice in the radio saying, "Slow down a little—there's another car coming at the next crossroad. . . . Better take route 29 because the main road is icy for a few miles. . . . Please report in when you get to Smith's Corners so I can check your cruising speed . . . etc." You would also be grateful for the fact that other drivers were being guided in the same rigid manner and that their precise location was known at all times to the man in the control room. However, with such procedures, we would hardly have thirty million automobiles on our highways.

Federal aviation authorities have already taken official cognizance of the helicopter's unusual attributes that make it possible for a person to stop in flight and think things over. Study is now being given to the possibility of revising air-traffic rules, pilots' physical requirements, and flight tests.

But the flight test of the future will probably not compare with the one I took for my helicopter rating in March, 1942. My good friend, Glenn L. Brown, Senior Aeronautical Inspector for the Civil Aeronautics Authority, scratched his head for a long time as he gazed at the little VS-300.

"How am I going to give you a test in that thing?" he demanded. "I can't ride with you; and even if I could, I wouldn't know whether you were flying it right or not. I tell you what. You just go up and show me your bag of tricks, and I'll try to think up some good ones before you land."

I gave the usual demonstration while he and Lloyd Proeb-sting, resident CAA inspector, looked on. Two or three times, they got their heads together in busy conference, and I knew they were working out some plans.

I landed in the middle of a fifteen-foot square, marked by strips of canvas on the ground, and they walked toward the ship with as much official dignity as they could assume under the circumstances.

"That 'airport' of yours is too big," said Brown; "and, besides, when you were up there buzzing around, we couldn't tell whether you were flying the ship or the ship was flying you! Now, take off and make some figure-eights around pylons. Proebsting and I will be one pylon; you pick out any spot in the field for the other one. Make them accurate, and don't lose or gain altitude"—this last with a chuckle. I was making the turns twenty feet high, so there wasn't much altitude to lose.

"Then, when you come in," he continued, "show us a real precision landing. You see this canvas strip here," pointing to the edge of my "airport"; "land with the seat right over the strip, and with the wheels equidistant from the ends of it!"

The "eights" were performed as usual and seemed to pass muster. So I made the spot landing astraddle the canvas and waited while Brown sighted along one side, then along the other, then measured the distance of the wheels from the ends of the strip.

At last he shook his head. "You couldn't do it a second time!" he said. So I took off and repeated the process.

"You win," he laughed. "Guess I'll have to give you the rating."

Thus was concluded the first Federal flight test for a helicopter license, and I received the first commercial helicopter rating that was ever, to my knowledge, issued. Unfortunately for the record, however, my original certificate number

(7917) had to be carried along, but the priority nevertheless holds good.

A few months later, Mr. Sikorsky applied to Brown for a Federal *private* pilot rating. Apparently Brown had been doing a bit of thinking, and he arrived with a formidable list of maneuvers for Mr. Sikorsky to demonstrate! As would be expected, he took the test in his stride and came through with flying colors, thus adding the first Federal private helicopter license to his many other "firsts."

Obviously, the future flight tests will be more fully developed than the ones we were required to take. Nevertheless, they will doubtless be attuned to the helicopter's own peculiar qualities. According to present indications, the CAA should have the tests, the physical requirements, and the flight regulations well formulated by the time helicopters even begin to emerge into general use.

In May, 1943, the XR-4, with Gregory at the controls, demonstrated for the first time the practicability of landing on shipboard. As a joint project of the War Shipping Administration and the Army Air Forces, the tanker *S.S. Bunker Hill* was fitted with a small deck amidships. The area available for landing was 60 by 78 feet. It was clear at the sides, but the bridge was at the forward end, and the aft end was marked by a tall mast with numerous stays and cables. When the vessel was under way, the air coming around the bridge was turbulent and treacherous, adding immeasurably to the test of the helicopter's precision control and rough-weather handling in such close quarters.

As we cruised about Long Island Sound, the wind on the deck would change direction and velocity, sometimes being strong over the bow, sometimes moderate on the beam, and sometimes light from astern. Our speed varied up to as much as sixteen knots. The XR-4 operated in all these conditions,

OPERATING IN AND OUT OF A SMALL BOAT ANCHORAGE.

MR. SIKORSKY LANDS AMONG PARKED CARS.

COL. H. F. GREGORY PREPARES TO LAND THE XR-4 ON THE DECK OF THE S.S. BUNKER HILL.

TIGHT QUARTERS.

THE AUTHOR IN THE VS-300 STRADDLES A WIDE CRACK BETWEEN TWO ENGINE BOXES.

and Gregory did a masterful job of piloting, occasionally making a tailfirst take-off, then again going straight up along the mast, or sliding out sideways over the churning water.

Twenty-three landings and take-offs were made. The trials were an eminent success and paved the way for further investigations of the helicopter's potentialities for convoy work, operating from small platforms on merchant vessels.

However, one feature remained to be checked: What would be the story if the surface vessel were rolling or pitching in a heavy sea? With this question in mind, the Army fitted a deck 56 by 62 feet to the *S.S. James Parker* and we set out, early in July, for a three-day cruise in the open ocean. This time, the deck was at the stern, and we had two helicopters aboard—the XR-4, operating on wheels, and one of the YR-4A's on pontoons.

There were five pilots: Gregory and Cooper; two recent students of mine, Lt. H. H. Hermes and Lt. F. W. Peterson; and myself. Between us, we managed to keep the ships in the air most of the time.

Since our chief purpose was to secure information on rough-weather flights, we were somewhat disappointed that the sea remained generally quite placid. One day, however, we had a moderate roll and it didn't seem to handicap the operations; so, pending the results of more complete tests, we tentatively concluded that the helicopter may be able to meet considerably less favorable conditions without too much trouble.

On thinking back over the life of our helicopter to date, one is struck by the amazing rapidity with which progress has been made.

Only five years ago, the VS-300 was non-existent. Now it is a museum piece, with all the honor and glory that is accorded a trail blazer. Hard on its heels came the XR-4,

ACA 349
(Rev. 9-1-40)

UNITED STATES OF AMERICA
DEPARTMENT OF COMMERCE
CIVIL AERONAUTICS ADMINISTRATION
WASHINGTON

AIRMAN CERTIFICATE NO. 7917

This certifies that  CHARLES L. MORRIS  is properly qualified
and is physically able to perform the duties of  COMMERCIAL PILOT

Address  PUTNEY RD., STRATFORD, CONN.

*Reinstated 3/16/42, [signature]*

| DATE OF BIRTH | WEIGHT | HEIGHT | HAIR | EYES | SEX |
|---|---|---|---|---|---|
| 10/20/08 | 160 | 6' | LT. BROWN | BLUE | MALE |

THIS CERTIFICATE is of 60 days' duration and, unless the holder hereof is otherwise notified within such period, shall continue in effect indefinitely thereafter, unless suspended or revoked by the Civil Aeronautics Board, except that it shall immediately expire (1) at the end of each SIX months' period after the date of issuance hereof if the holder of this certificate fails to secure an endorsement by an authorized inspector within the last 45 days of each such period, or (2) at any time an authorized inspector shall refuse to endorse this certificate after inspection or examination.

Endorsement Refused

Date: _____

Date of Issuance  MARCH 16, 1942
By direction of the Administrator:

Signature: _____

Title: SENIOR AERONAUTICAL INSPECTOR

Inspector, Civil Aeronautics Administration

This certificate is not valid unless there is attached hereto the appropriate Rating Record bearing the above number. Any alteration of this certificate is punishable by a fine of not exceeding $1,000 or imprisonment not exceeding three years, or both.

Signature of Holder: _____

---

Form ACA 545
(Rev. 11-1-40)

UNITED STATES OF AMERICA
DEPARTMENT OF COMMERCE
CIVIL AERONAUTICS ADMINISTRATION
WASHINGTON

AIRMAN RATING RECORD NO. 7917

This Rating Record is not valid unless accompanied by the appropriate certificate bearing the above number.

Name  CHARLES L. MORRIS
Address  PUTNEY RD., STRATFORD, CONN.

RATINGS WITH LIMITATIONS

HELICOPTER

By direction of the Administrator:

_____
(Civil Aeronautics Inspector)

MARCH 16, 1942
(Date of Issuance)

Any change of address should be endorsed on reverse side hereof but only after written notice has been mailed to the Certificate Division, Civil Aeronautics Administration, Washington, D. C. Any alteration of this form may result in the suspension or revocation of the Certificate to which this form is attached.

FIRST COMMERCIAL HELICOPTER PILOT RATING.

to astonish a world and set countless records and "firsts," as well as to establish an enviable reputation for rugged, rigorous service. The two ships together, in company with their creator, fired the public's imagination beyond all bounds. And now we have the XR-5 and the XR-6 with their own packets of surprises waiting to be announced.

Four years ago, if someone had said to you, "Are you going to own a helicopter when they come on the market?" you probably would have responded, "What in heaven's name *is* a 'helicopter'?" Today, if your after-dinner conversation turns to helicopters and someone in the group fails to show enthusiasm, you probably dub him backward and uninformed.

All this has come about in such a short space of time. The war has certainly helped to expedite it, but even if the war had not come, I am certain those responsible for the helicopter would have carried it forward with the same enthusiasm, courage, and ability.

Tremendous strides have been made. Even greater strides are this minute in the making. Much that was unknown or surmised a year ago has now been broken down, analyzed, studied, and applied with greater understanding.

Much more still remains behind a veil that can be raised only by further research, experimentation, and experience.

It is pertinent, then, to ask, "What of the future?"

*Chapter XIII*

## PROPHECY AND WARNING

THE YEAR 1944 WAS STILL IN ITS SWADDLING CLOTHES when a Sikorsky helicopter performed a lifesaving mission that was totally spontaneous and tragically necessary. It was the first completely unstaged job, and as such was an augury of an ever-expanding future in transportation and service.

On January 3, a Navy destroyer exploded off Sandy Hook, New Jersey. Men were killed, injured, burned, and many suffered from shock. Blood plasma was needed urgently and quickly. By boat from the Battery it would take over an hour to cross the bay. By car it would be necessary to follow a roundabout route on icy roads through New Jersey, taking even longer than the boat trip.

The Coast Guard Air Base at Floyd Bennett Field in lower Brooklyn had some Sikorsky helicopters. Commander Frank A. Erickson, one of my students, was in charge of the base. He secured flight clearance, even though all other military and commercial aircraft were grounded by very low clouds, freezing rain and snow, and high winds. He landed at the Battery, picked up the plasma, and finished the job more quickly than could have been accomplished by any other means.

*The New York Times*, two days later, carried what I consider the best editorial on the subject that could possibly have been written. It is quoted in full:

### HELICOPTER TO THE RESCUE

Dramatic in its setting and purpose was the demonstration of the practical utility of the helicopter in aid of men wounded by the destroyer explosion off Sandy Hook. Through snow squalls and sleet which kept all other types of aircraft grounded, Comdr. Frank A. Erickson, head of the Coast Guard aviation unit at Floyd Bennett Field, had no difficulty in taking off one of the experimental heli- copters from that station and landing it at the Battery. Fourteen minutes later it settled gently on the beach at Sandy Hook with two cases of blood plasma for the survivors of the explosion.

The forty units were rushed to hospitals and immediately admin- istered. To deliver this lifesaving shipment by boat would have taken an hour; by car, an hour and a half. Commander Erickson, who promptly flew his whirligig aircraft back to his post, called it merely a "routine operation." It was indeed routine for the strange rotary- winged machine which Igor Sikorsky has brought to practical flight, but it shows in striking fashion how the helicopter can make use of tiny landing areas in conditions of visibility which make other types of flying impossible.

The helicopter is proving its value in war. Its peacetime uses are obvious. There remain technical difficulties of vibration and control which must be overcome in its development. We should not expect to see these machines buzzing commuters to work all over the land immediately after the war is over. But it should be clear that noth- ing can dim the future for a machine which can take in its stride weather conditions such as those which prevailed in New York on Monday.

Thus, the *Times* recognized the immediate potentialities of the helicopter. At the same time, it sounded a thoughtful warning against over-optimism, saying, in effect, "Don't think that, just because the helicopter is fulfilling a vital military purpose today, John Doe will be buying and flying one to- morrow for his day-to-day pursuits." Nevertheless, since John Doe wants to believe in the helicopter as a potentially great post-war industry that will affect his own existence, he has a strong desire to disregard conservative warnings.

In an effort to combat his attitude, many informed writers and speakers have swung to the other extreme with over- pessimistic statements. It seems to me that the correct path lies between the two. It is proposed, in closing this book, to discuss a few salient points in a realistic manner so that the reader may be better prepared to separate the wheat from the chaff and to draw his own well-thought-out conclusions.

Perhaps the subject on which there has been the greatest amount of loose, unfounded comment is the price for which a helicopter may be bought after the war. In the *Atlantic Monthly* for September, 1942, Mr. Sikorsky made a statement that was carefully considered and that said exactly what he meant to say—no more, no less. It was: "Manufactured by hundreds of thousands, the helicopter will cost about as much as a medium-priced automobile."

Since then, helicopter publicity has indulged in some luscious wishful thinking, coming to a climax in a recent promise made by someone who had everything to gain and nothing to lose, that a post-war helicopter would sell for $995—not $996 or $994—but exactly $995!

Let us endeavor to inject some sanity into this business of guessing at a price.

To begin with, can you confidently assert what a dollar will be worth after the war? Will a pair of shoes cost $6 or $2 or $20—or perhaps even more? Will a low-priced car still sell for $800?

With uncertainty as to the value of the dollar, it is downright foolishness to promise a fixed price for anything. Estimates should be made relative to some other commodity. That is why Mr. Sikorsky chose to compare the helicopter with "a medium-priced automobile." If a medium-priced automobile should sell for $6,000 after the war, this prophecy would still be within shooting distance.

But care should even be exercised in interpreting that word *medium-priced*. It definitely does not mean *average-priced*. On the basis of pre-war dollar values, a high-priced automobile costs about $3,000 to $4,000; a low-priced one, about $900 to $1,000. Therefore, medium-priced means something in the neighborhood of $2,000 to $2,500. But let me emphasize again that dollar signs should not appear in this discussion. The safest statement is that, *if* a $2,200 pre-war car still sells for $2,200 after the war, then, under certain circumstances, a helicopter may someday sell for about the same price.

What are those "certain circumstances"? Mr. Sikorsky says: "manufactured by hundreds of thousands." That sounds simple, perhaps—but it isn't. Before our entrance into the war, the President shocked the aircraft industry by establishing a quota of 50,000 airplanes for a twelve-month period. This was more than all the airplanes we had ever built since the Wright brothers flew at Kittyhawk!

But note carefully that it was the responsibility of an *entire* industry to meet that figure. It did—by virtue of a perfectly tremendous effort.

Recent releases indicate that at present this country is producing about 9,000 airplanes a month. And when I say "this country," I mean all that it implies. After four hard years, a great, nationwide industry, expanded to many times its pre-war size, utilizing vast facilities of the automotive field, and working under extremes of war pressure with the maximum of priority, still has a cumulative output of only about 100,000 units a year—and even those units are divided among about forty different types of aircraft.

If it has taken four years to accomplish this, how long will it take one individual company to reach the same production figure—much less the "hundreds of thousands" Mr. Sikorsky referred to? The answer is self-evident, at least in negation: it will *not* be soon after the war!

The situation back of Mr. Sikorsky's statement might be clarified if it is realized that the automotive industry generally builds engines for about a dollar per horsepower. Aircraft engines, on the other hand, average about ten times this amount, although some have cut the horsepower costs to around $5 to $6. When we consider that a satisfactory two- to three-place helicopter should have about 200-horsepower, it immediately becomes apparent that the engine alone is going to cost as much as the optimists are planning to pay for the whole machine! Mass production may come to the rescue later on, but it is probable that, for quite a while, aircraft engines will continue to be higher priced than automobile engines. If you proceed further and apply this type of analysis to the transmission, the main-rotor and tail-rotor blades, the hub mechanisms, the controls, the instruments, the landing gear, and the fuselage structure itself, you begin to appreciate Mr. Sikorsky's reasoning when he said: "Manufactured by hundreds of thousands, it will cost about as much as a medium-priced automobile."

What about performance: speed, range, and load? Here I always tread cautiously and surround each statement with carefully guarded qualifications. I remember that, about 1928, an eminent aeronautical engineer prepared and published an erudite dissertation proving conclusively that an airplane weighing more than 30,000 pounds could never leave the ground. Yet we now see airplanes of two to three times that size, and we confidently expect them to exceed 100 tons, or even 500 tons, when the economic need arises. The fallacy of the 1928 forecast was that it did not take into account future research and development. If it had started by saying, "On the basis of present knowledge . . . ," it would have been on tenable ground.

In surveying the helicopter's future, that qualifying phrase assumes even greater significance. All through this book it is apparent that the astounding successes were achieved with a most elementary knowledge of the machine. Helicopter research is practically nil compared with the vast amount that has been done on the conventional airplanes. As the fund of knowledge grows, the entire outlook cannot but change accordingly.

It should be remembered, also, that this book has dealt only with one type of helicopter comprising essentially a single main rotor with torque-compensating tail rotor. Research may reveal other types as being ultimately more practical— or it may develop some completely undreamed-of mechanical means of doing the job that would make our present thinking as out-of-date as a 1910 automobile.

Therefore, we arrive at two fundamental protective phrases: (1) "on the basis of present knowledge" and (2) "with the present type of machine." Performance estimates made with those reservations may be of interest.

Thus far, the XR-4 has achieved a speed upward of eighty miles an hour in level flight. This is not fast, and a glance at a picture of the craft will reveal, even to an untrained eye, many places where speed could be increased by better streamlining. We have reason to believe that helicopters will shortly exceed 110 to 120 miles per hour.

Going back to Mr. Sikorsky's *Atlantic Monthly* article, we find a prediction of 140 miles an hour for the more distant future. But that is as far as common sense permits us now to think. Research, or a different type of machine, may extend this limit. If so, we may consider it an unexpected dividend. In the meantime, the speed in hand can and will have plenty of useful applications.

As for load, we shouldn't seek too much. A capacity of eight to twelve passengers appears well within range. An ultimate of twenty passengers is perhaps a reasonable guess. But I am not revealing any secrets when I say that, for best performance, a helicopter should not carry much more than ten pounds per horsepower. (The fact that we have done considerable flying with more than fourteen pounds per horsepower does not alter the basic truth of this statement, because we sacrificed other good qualities in the interest of load.) About six or seven of those ten pounds will be structural weight. Therefore, we end up with a balance of three or four pounds per horsepower that can be applied to passengers, fuel, oil, and baggage.

Twenty passengers, plus baggage, weigh about 4,000 pounds. Adding the fuel and oil necessary for a reasonable flight, we deduce that somewhere around 2,000 horsepower will be required for a twenty-passenger ship. A 2,000-horsepower helicopter may not be impossible, but it is certainly a long step ahead of what we have so far achieved. Therefore, we are quite content to establish that as our first goal—let come what may thereafter.

Non-stop flying range is, of course, a factor of load. If you wanted to carry, in gasoline, the equivalent of twenty passengers, you could fly solo far enough to get quite bored with yourself. On the other hand, you could probably carry thirty or more people for a fairly short flight, by the simple expedient of not filling the gas tanks so full. When we speak of load, however, we automatically figure on giving the helicopter enough gas to fly for three or four hours—which means somewhere around 300 to 500 miles, non-stop. This is comparable to standard airplane practice; and a helicopter with such characteristics would be a useful vehicle.

So, "on the basis of present knowledge, and with the present type of machine," I feel confident in prophesying satisfactory performance in speed, load, and range. If you don't consider it satisfactory, you are entitled to await the results of the next several years—or do your own guessing.

What about that question of controls? One technically qualified commentator has stated that the operating of a helicopter requires a greater degree of skill than does an airplane and far greater skill than does a car. He estimates that it will take between five and ten years of further study before the controls will become sufficiently simplified to make the craft suitable for public use.

I am in no position to argue the first part of his statement. If he cares to suggest that I am skillful, I bow a grateful acknowledgment. But I must take issue with his conclusion. There are only two difficulties that stand in the way of simplifying the present controls. One is the need for applying our entire efforts in other directions. The second is the need for deciding whether the ultimate helicopter controls should be more like those of an automobile or of an airplane. Once the latter decision has been reached, and once we can spend a little time on the matter, I believe that great simplification could be introduced almost overnight.

Persons accustomed to automotive thinking often ask, "How many miles do you get on a gallon of gas?" In aviation, "miles per gallon" is changed to read "gallons per hour." If a certain airplane uses ten gallons of gas an hour, and cruises at 120, it will be going twelve miles to the gallon. But, if it hits a head wind, or rides along on a tail wind, the amount of gas consumed per mile may be greatly affected. That is why aviation does not think in automotive terms, but refers instead to the gasoline used every hour, regardless of distance covered.

An engine developing a certain power will burn a certain amount of gas per hour, whether it be in a helicopter, an airplane, or a rowboat (atmospheric conditions being equal). Therefore, before deciding how economical a helicopter will be, we have to decide what horsepower we are planning to use.

The chances are that a good two-place helicopter would have about 200 horsepower. It would be about a 2,000-pound machine, including passengers, baggage, and gasoline. It would probably cruise about 100 miles an hour (maybe faster when we learn more) and burn about eleven gallons of gas for every hour in the air. This would give us about nine miles to the gallon on the average.

Before you make too many mental comparisons with your fifteen-miles-per-gallon automobile, bear in mind that when you drive somewhere by car, you often go several miles farther than the distance as the crow flies. So the helicopter, cutting across lots, will save somewhat on the actual mileage of the trip. Bear in mind also that your car will be running about three times as long as the helicopter for any given trip —which means three times the wear and tear on the mechanism. And, finally, for each mile your car travels, you are paying a quarter of a cent for tires—which will probably never wear out at all on a helicopter.

Taking all these things into consideration, the comparison is not so unfavorable as it may at first appear—and by the time you charge off a little for time saved, for enjoyment, and for flexibility, the scales swing definitely toward the helicopter.

If you already have some background knowledge of aviation, you probably wonder why the two-place helicopter requires nearly twice as much horsepower as a two-place airplane. The answer lies in the fundamental truth that you cannot get something for nothing. If you are going to want zero air speed, vertical take-off, and hovering at places that are six or eight thousand feet high, you must have the power for it. Actually, I am not particularly concerned on this point, because I believe the utility of the helicopter will justify the larger engine.

Having thus openly discussed the present limitations of the helicopter, the conflict of Hope versus Fact may lead us to wonder just what the post-war era does hold in store. You will recall that I became associated with the helicopter in the beginning because its horizons appeared unlimited. The further we proceed, the more the outlook expands. I hope I may be permitted to conclude with a page or two of sober crystal gazing.

At the present time, and for the immediate future, the helicopter is in the same category as refrigerators, radios, automobiles, and everything else that you cannot buy now. How soon these commodities may again appear on the civilian market will be determined solely by the progress of the war—and my crystal is clouded in this regard.

At the conclusion of hostilities, we shall emerge with some helicopter models, evolved or evolving, that will readily lend themselves to many specialized uses. They will cost a lot of money—I won't estimate how much, because even if dollar values could be relied upon, the price is heavily contingent upon the quantity of production that will have then been achieved, and this in turn largely depends on the duration of the war. Nevertheless, it is a safe assumption that they will be expensive, and therefore restricted to particular jobs where initial cost is not a primary factor. They will probably be operated by mining and oil companies prospecting areas that were hitherto inaccessible, such as the jungles of South America or the waste lands of Canada; by geologists and explorers; by airlines and bus companies creating new routes or providing more adequate coverage on old ones; by business establishments (hotels, newspapers, department stores, etc.), capitalizing on the up-to-the-minute service that the helicopter can render; by concerns engaged in crop dusting, surveying, aerial photography, and similar agricultural and industrial assignments; by the Red Cross and other humanitarian enterprises for floods, blizzards, hurricanes, and disasters of all sorts; and, finally, by government agencies for police work, forest and fire patrol, lifesaving, and emergency missions of a thousand unpredictable types. These are only a few striking examples of the jobs for which the helicopter of today is entirely suited and that would be economically practical almost without regard to what its original purchase price would have to be.

Bit by bit, production quantities and practices could develop to the point where costs would begin to drop. Other buyers could then afford them for less specialized purposes. As these demands are met, prices could again be reduced; and once the snowball is started, it could gather momentum surprisingly quickly, bringing costs down to the point where the helicopter might at last be considered on the "public market."

The first two steps, though—military use and specialized commercial use—must of necessity cover a period of years. The period may be somewhat reduced if post-war markets justify tooling up for a pre-established output (10,000, 20,000, 50,000 per year) and counting on the sales department to clear the shelves. This would be a new experience to aviation, which has generally not produced much ahead of orders. But even if such a step were taken, it would still be several years after the war before a medium-priced helicopter became a reality.

In any such forecast of the future, there are so many intangibles that it is safest to indicate them clearly—and then retire to await the ultimate and inevitable solution.

One thing is certain—the helicopter is here to stay. It will have its ups and downs, its protagonists and antagonists. But it has unalterably become a part of our future existence. How soon you as an individual may benefit from its services is beyond the power of anyone now to prophesy.

# REFERENCES

This listing comprises a few articles and books that give further background for the helicopter, including some that provide Autogiro information of particular interest.

DE LA CIERVA, JUAN, and ROSE, DON: "Wings of Tomorrow," Brewer, Warren & Putnam, New York, 1931.

GREGORY, COL. H. F.: "Army's Flying Windmill," *Air Force*, March, 1943.

"Helicopters of Tomorrow, Interview with I. I. Sikorsky," *Aviation*, January, 1942.

KASTNER, J.: "Sikorsky's Helicopter," *Life*, June 21, 1943.

KLEMIN, ALEXANDER: "Principles of Rotary Aircraft," *Journal of the Franklin Institute*, February and March, 1939.

LE PAGE, W. LAURENCE: "Flight on Rotating Wing," *Journal of the Franklin Institute*, September and October, 1936.

MORRIS, C. L.: "Dawn of a New Era," *Air Force*, March, 1943.

MORRIS, C. L.: "Dream Come True," *Air Facts*, April, 1943.

SIKORSKY, I. I.: "Progress of the Vought-Sikorsky Helicopter Program in 1942," *Aeronautical Engineering Review*, April, 1943.

SIKORSKY, I. I.: "Story of the Winged-S," Dodd, Mead & Co., New York, 1938.

SIKORSKY, I. I.: "Technical Development of the VS-300 Helicopter during 1941," *Journal of the Aeronautical Sciences*, June, 1942.